Praise...
Four Years, Two Roads

Derek has been blessed with a God-given passion and burdened with a vital responsibility to bring young people closer to the heart of God. His authentic and transparent faith, clearly shown through this work, is an inspiration to many, including myself!

— **Kirk Cousins NFL Quarterback,**
Author of *Game Changer: Faith, Football, & Finding Your Way*

Derek Kim is on a mission: to make sure that today's high school students know they have a choice during their teenage years: they *can* do the right thing, they *can* choose Christ. This is a much needed book and dialogue, and Kim is well positioned, as a young person himself, to encourage our youth that standing apart because of your faith or lifestyle choices isn't something to be ashamed of. Young people need a voice and they need to feel they're not alone. This work accomplishes both.

— **Kirsten Haglund**
Miss America 2008

Derek has created the MacGyver of books for students to navigate high school while walking with Jesus! This book is real, relevant, and reliable! I'm thankful for how it will lead students to live for Jesus across the country!

— **E.J. Swanson**
Nationally Recognized Christian Speaker and Tour Pastor

Four Years, Two Roads addresses a dire need in American youth culture. Derek Kim effectively explains both why and how students can still choose the harder, narrower road and serve their Lord and Savior Jesus Christ. Young saints will leave reading Kim's book eager to delight in God. This is a valuable resource for any young Christian. I wish it had been available when I was in high school!

— Chris Norman
Michigan State Football Captain and Linebacker
(testimony featured on desiringgod.org)

Derek has hit a home run for high school students with this book. All who read it will be better suited to not only strive after Christ, but achieve eternal success. I'm inspired by Derek, and I know that Four Years, Two Roads will be a difference maker for high school students everywhere.

— Tim Shaw
Tennessee Titans Linebacker

Four Years, Two Roads

Finding Eternal Significance
in High School

Derek Kim

Clay's,
Thank you for being
faithful to God's Word!
Y'all are an encouragement
to me.

Galatians 6-9-10

Concerning Life Publishing

Cover Designed by Molli Krick and Mattie Ozment

Edited by Rachelle Rea (www.RachelleRea.com)

Kim, Derek
Four Years, Two Roads

Finding Eternal Significance in High School

ISBN-10:0988922592
ISBN-13:978-0-9889225-9-4

Library of Congress Control Number: 2014932289

Concerning Life Publishing
16282 Gierman Dr.
Spring Lake, MI 49456

Acknowledgments

Wow, am I really finished? Staying up until 4 a.m. throughout my first few years of college, I thought I would never make it. But God is faithful. In the book of Joshua, the waters of the Jordan did not recede until the Israelites stepped *in* the river. We have to push while we pray. And we must never cease to marvel at how God displays His faithfulness in tandem with our obedience.

The church—God's elect—is the most powerful institution this world has ever seen. The Body of Christ is what made this book possible, of which I will now name the few I have had the pleasure of partnering with in this project.

Molli Krick and Mattie Ozment, thank you for creating an awesome, creative cover. I know it is not easy being a student athlete and taking on other obligations.

To my editors, Kim Koilpillai and Rachelle Rea, your attention to detail was tremendous. Thank you for being encouraging and honest.

To my high school youth pastor and small group leader Jack Janigian and Todd George, the investment of your time and resources into my life during high school made this book possible. Not just on Wednesdays at 7:07 p.m., but the countless phone conversations, dinners, lunches, mission trips, retreats, and Bible studies. Thank you, old men.

My dear brothers in the faith Connor Smith, Kuni Hotta, and Chris Norman, words cannot express how thankful I am for you. Your suggestions sharpened my thoughts. Your prayers drove me through discouragement. I once asked the Lord for brothers who would spur me on to good deeds. I have received that and so much more.

I can't forget about my sisters in Christ! Allison Gudeman, Victoria Clay, Allie Vogel, my wonderful prom date, Elizabeth Maier, and Lakin Pratt, the coolest southern belle ever—I am grateful for your generous input. Your desires to embrace Biblical femininity shine ever so brightly in this dark world.

Perry and Sarah Dunlap, thank you for modeling to me and so many others the extravagant drama of marriage. I am thankful God put couples like you two in my life who are more knowledgeable in relationships than I am. Your contribution into the dating chapter was tremendous.

I must also recognize some of my heroes in the faith.

To the Passion team—Louie Giglio, Francis Chan, John Piper—I love the 268 declaration. My heart beats with the rest of the 268 Generation. The exaltation of Jesus' name and His renown is the desire of my soul. There is no alternative. Because I refuse to waste my life.

As I write this two semesters away from graduation, the passion behind this book has not changed: to see the upcoming generation live unashamedly for the glory of Jesus Christ and Him crucified.

To *umma* and *abba*,
Thank you for teaching me the value of hard work and self-discipline.
I have found no greater example of Christ-like sacrifice.

Contents

Foreword
Andrew Maxwell

Chapter One Narrow-Minded

Chapter Two Make it a Priority: What I Would've Done
Differently

Chapter Three The Narrow Road Through Sports and
Extracurricular

Chapter Four Year One: Freshman Year

Chapter Five The Narrow Road Through Academics

Chapter Six Year Two: Sophomore Year

Chapter Seven The Narrow Road Through The Party Scene

Chapter Eight Year Three: Junior Year

Chapter Nine The Narrow Road Through Dating

Chapter Ten One of the Most Powerful Forces in the Universe

Chapter Eleven The Narrow Road Through Ministry

Chapter Twelve Year Four: Senior Year

Chapter Thirteen Good News

Chapter Fourteen The Real King

Foreword

On September 2nd, 2013, I was the starting quarterback for the Michigan State Spartans. On September 3rd, I wasn't.

After starting all thirteen games of the 2012 season and the opening game of the 2013 season, I was benched. The decision came after a 2012 season filled with adversity and disappointment, an offseason filled with controversy and questions, and an opening game void of much offensive production. As the lightning rod of the team, I was the aim of a growing wave of criticism and doubt, which came to a break that Tuesday afternoon in Coach Mark Dantonio's office as he informed me of his decision to go in a different direction at the quarterback position.

Sitting in that chair I found myself at the intersection of two roads: one narrow, one wide.

In the following three or four weeks, I can't honestly say I traveled down either one. I would start down one and return to the intersection like I had forgotten something, only to head down the other and do the same thing. In order to truly enter through one of the two gates, I had to decide between not which journey was easiest or most attractive, but which destination was the most worthwhile.

Wide gates are wide for a reason. People enter through them because they are attractive to the immediate senses. There is usually little thought to the destination or reward at the end of the road. This is why wide gates are dangerous. They beckon and call with the promise of satisfaction and fulfillment. But wide gates are liars. Wide gates lead to wide roads, which lead to false gods, disappointments and a wasted life.

Blame. Anger. Frustration. Bitterness. These were what invited me down the wide road, and I would be lying if I said they weren't attractive. They were easy. Dare I say they were natural? These I wrestled with for weeks, a boxing match between my flesh and the Spirit.

I can't tell you an exact date, but eventually the Lord turned my gaze from the broad road to the narrow destination—from the journey to the end. While contemplating the wide gate, I focused only on what was easy, only on the road, but I did not see that Jesus clearly points out that its end is destruction (Matthew 7:13). In verse 14, while highlighting the contrasting narrow road, Jesus offers no favors to those who focus solely on the journey and the road. He says the way is hard and that characteristic is why few find it. The flesh wants to tune out after that and not listen to the destination—life.

It was helpful for me to contrast Matthew 7:13-14 with a popular teaching of Jesus in Matthew 11:28. At first glance, it looks like a contradiction. Jesus says the way is hard, but then invites people who are weary and burdened. But what is the difference? The *way* is hard, but *Jesus* makes it worth it. The narrow road is difficult, but its destination is eternal satisfaction and rest.

I recently shared with my girlfriend that I was almost becoming annoyed because the narrow road I had chosen my senior year surprised and impressed so many people. People often complimented my "great faith" to handle the situation the way I did. I wasn't annoyed at the sincerity of their gestures; I was only agitated that in some instances I was being made the hero when, in reality, I was traveling the only road that makes sense as a Christian. I would be a fraud if I call myself a follower of Christ and then respond to a difficult situation with bitterness, blame, and anger. I would be a sham if I became divisive in the locker room. I would be a joke if my eternal joy was lost with the absence of my starting position.

I am not a hero for entering through the narrow gate. I am simply a pilgrim on a hard (but infinitely worthy) journey toward a beautiful, all-sufficient destination in Jesus.

When I first met Derek Kim in the fall of 2011, there was something noticeably different about him. The way he talked, the things he stood for, and the passion in his heart were not standard procedure for the average college freshman. It was clear Derek had been following Jesus through high school and it had changed everything about his life. I did not know Derek before college, but I don't need to have known him then to know that he is the perfect person to write a book on this topic. I have witnessed the result of his following Christ through high school and, it challenged, convicted, and encouraged me from day one. His choosing of the narrow gate has impacted people from Novi to East Lansing, from Lusaka, Zambia, to Johannesburg, South Africa, and even his home country of Seoul, South Korea—a true testimony to the Lord's faithful use of someone who submits himself to a hard road of eternal purpose.

Hebrews 13:7 tells us to remember those who taught us, consider the outcome of their way of life, and imitate their faith. That is my prayer for you as you read Four Years, Two Roads.

As a dear friend (and biblically speaking, brother) of Derek's, I have seen firsthand how Derek's choice to enter through the narrow gate and follow Jesus has led to nothing short of a life of eternal significance. This book is a tangible representation of his heart for those in this critical season of life and his deep yearning for students not to waste their one and only high school experience. I entreat you to take his words to heart, prayerfully consider the outcomes of walking the narrow road in high school, and be eternally satisfied—as well as pleasantly surprised—with the reward you find at the end: an inexhaustible fountain of life in our great God and King.

-Andrew Maxwell
Michigan State Quarterback 2009-2014

Introduction
How It All Started

I never thought I would get emotional in the conference room of a Holiday Inn.

After spending the past week serving the people of inner-city Detroit with 200 other high school students, Jack, our youth pastor, asked if any seniors wanted to share something they learned in the past four years.

"Where do I even start?"

I raised my hand, and as I did, I looked around the room. Seven days ago, we were a haphazard blend of high school students. Now, I saw brothers and sisters with incredible potential to influence their schools for Christ. I had seen their hearts. Their passion inspired me throughout the week at Vacation Bible Schools and street projects in some of Detroit's roughest neighborhoods.

Imagine if they brought this same fervor back to their student bodies, I thought to myself.

Then my stomach sank. I wasn't going to be with this faith family much longer. College was less than three months away. This was one of the last opportunities I had to leave an impact on this group I loved. *Where do I even begin with all that I have learned in high school? How do I sum up four years in five minutes? It would literally take a book!*

Indeed, it would.

I told myself I wasn't going to cry; whom was I kidding? The tears started to fall immediately, as I poured out my heart to the underclassmen that would soon be upperclassmen, and the upperclassmen that would soon be freshmen in college.

"Living for Christ in high school isn't the popular route, but if you're willing to be uncommon for His Kingdom cause, you can walk away from these four years with eternal satisfaction and zero regrets," I said.

Then, I shared my vision for what you now hold in your hand.

About a month prior to my final Detroit Mission Trip, my principal handed me my diploma at the Convocation Center of Eastern Michigan University. As I delivered my commencement speech to my classmates, I sensed that I wasn't done with high school quite yet.

I still had a message to share with the next generation.

Much has changed in the past few years. One thing that hasn't is my passion to see you—a high school student—live for Jesus.

I'm thrilled I get to share that with you.

The Unexpected Adventure

I never thought I would write a book.

I am 20 years old. English is my second language. Reading comprehension was among my worst standardized test scores. However, I have discovered that God takes you on all sorts of unexpected adventures when you decide to follow Him.

Today, it seems like most high school students are in a hurry to grow up and go to college. Perhaps this is you. You might be puzzled why someone would even write a book about high school. I got a similar response when I told people about my project: "Don't waste your time."

But for the young person who yearns to live out his or her Christian faith, these years are a cornerstone for the future. They are not a nuisance. They are a catapult for your years as a college student, young adult, and so forth.

But the numbers sure aren't rosy.

According to a study by Barna Group, 43 percent of teenagers disappear from the church after they graduate from high school[i]. So think about your youth group. According to research, half of the people you know from Bible study, small group, and your weekly meetings, won't be walking with the Lord after they graduate. You always have to be generous with statistics. However, I discovered there's a lot of truth to this number. The older I got, the more opposition I encountered in my Christian faith, from classmates, coaches, science teachers, and the culture we live in. It was discouraging, even depressing at times. But a truth in Jesus' Sermon on the Mount became an anchor for my soul. Living for Jesus never has and never will be popular—especially in high school. Jesus guaranteed His followers suffering. Yet, why did His 12 disciples still leave behind their families, jobs, and reputations to follow Him?

Because He is worth it.

Chapter One
Narrow-Minded

Something is Missing

My four years of high school were the best years of my life thus far. As I write this, I am a few weeks away from leaving for Michigan State University, where I will start another exciting chapter of my life. Trust me, I am ready to move on, but high school will remain a memorable part of my life, and that is how I feel it should be.

However, as I have observed my peers now that we have graduated, this way of thinking does not seem to be all too common. Many have told me that they hated high school and that these were some of the worst years of their lives.

This concerns me.

Hate high school? Worst years of their lives? What is so bad about being a teenager and enjoying all the opportunities that God has given you?

The more I heard these things; the more I realized that many students fail to utilize their opportunities during some of the most influential years of their lives. Ecclesiastes 11:9 says, *"Be happy, young man, while you are young, and let your heart give you joy in the days of your youth."* God never meant for us to be in a hurry to grow up. He wants us to take advantage of the opportunities we have in every season of life. Sadly, this does not seem to be the attitude of the typical student.

What Really Matters?

As I grew up, I as well was tempted to fall into the trap of believing what the world says: our identity and satisfaction is found in our successes, dreams, and approval of others. Guys think they need to be athletic to get all the girls, and be a real man. Ladies feel that they need to change whom they are, and how they look, to have value.

That's a bunch of crap.

At the end of your life, it's not going to matter how many awards you won or how popular you were. The only thing that will matter is if you had a relationship with Jesus, and how that faith led you to make an impact in the lives of others.

At every funeral I attend, people talk about relationships. What did this person give back to the world? What kind of influence did he or she have on other people? People are remembered by what they give *to* the world, not by what they take *from* it. Because when we die, we are not going to take anything with us.

Some have told me that high school students are too young to think about such matters; that's ridiculous! In fact, it's because these matters aren't pondered enough that many students are in the predicament they are in. The decisions you make as a teenager reflect the choices you will make 20 or 30 years down the road. Yes, you are "only" in high school, but these are some of the most critical years of your life. Yes, you are "only" in high school, but this is the time to take a stand for what you believe in. Yes, you are "only" in high school; it is time to start thinking about more than varsity letters and homecoming dates.

I am writing this book because I am concerned. The majority of high school students are going along with the status quo, believing the world's lies, and as a result, wasting some of the most influential years of their lives. Life is short; there's only a limited amount of time to leave an impact. John Piper said it so powerfully in his life changing book *Don't Waste Your Life*,

"You don't have to know a lot of things for your life to make a lasting difference in the world. But you do have to know the few great things that matter, perhaps just one, and then be willing to live for them and die for them. The people that make a durable difference in the world are not the people who have mastered many things, but who have been mastered by one great thing. If you want your life to count, if you want the ripple effect of the pebbles you drop to become waves that reach the ends of the earth and roll on into eternity, you don't need to have a high IQ. You don't have to have good looks or riches or come from a fine family or a fine school. Instead you have to know a few great, majestic, unchanging, obvious, simple, glorious things—or one great all-embracing thing — and be set on fire by them."[ii]

Jesus is Worth it

I became a follower of Jesus Christ in seventh grade. As I transitioned from middle school to high school, the Lord granted me a holy ambition to boldly live for Him. I was in awe of the grace of God, how He had saved me from hell and offered me a life of eternal significance. Thus, I began to pore over His word, staying up late at night to learn more about Jesus' life and commandments.

The first verse I memorized was Romans 1:16, *"For I am not ashamed of the gospel, for it is the power of God for salvation to everyone who believes, to the Jew first and also to the Greek."* What is sad, though, is that more often than not, I *was* ashamed of the Gospel. Part of me wanted to live for Jesus, but another side of me also wanted to be popular and respected by everyone at school. "Father, please help me to live for you, but not lose any of my friends," I would pray.

Talk about an unanswered prayer.

That was just the beginning. The more I grew in my faith, the more resistance I encountered. I quickly found out that most of my classmates didn't really care about what I was learning at youth group.

Furthermore, I learned that if I was truly going to follow Jesus, it meant I was going to have to sacrifice some relationships.

Following Him comes with a cost. It's not the popular route. But in high school, I learned that the hard thing is usually the right thing. Emotions are deceiving, and the truth of God's word always trumps what "feels good" at the present moment. Some sacrifices have to be made, but when you contrast it with the joy of having a relationship with Jesus, there is no comparison.

Scripture complements Scripture. When you begin to connect the dots in God's Word, you quickly realize that His mind is far beyond ours. And that's a very good thing. "*I am not ashamed of the gospel,*" the Apostle Paul proclaims. Keeping in mind everything this guy went through—torture, famine, nakedness, threats, loss of social status, eventually martyrdom—what would motivate him to have zero regrets? I believe the answer comes in his letter to the church at Philippi; his words are also the reason why you can follow Jesus with no regrets.

> *Indeed, I count everything as loss because of the surpassing worth of knowing Christ Jesus my Lord. For his sake I have suffered the loss of all things and count them as rubbish in order that I may gain Christ.*
> —Philippians 3:8

Here's my favorite part of this verse: the word for "rubbish" isn't just referring to what you find in a garbage can. The original Greek word is *skybalon*, and it only appears here in the New Testament. *Skybalon* refers to rotten food, dung—literally, poop. Some scholars say it was used to describe half-eaten corpses and manure. So compared to knowing Jesus, Paul not only says that his past life is "poop," but that it was repulsive and harmful. Strong words, eh? What was true for Paul is also true for you, Christian. Our God is not some far-off being who doesn't want to be involved in our lives. Frankly, it's quite the opposite. We can *know* Christ personally as our Savior and Lord, and discover that God's acceptance trumps anything the world could offer.

But the road is narrow.

A "Good" Narrow-Mindedness

One of the most common responses I got when I shared my faith was that I was "narrow-minded".

"That's cool that the Bible works for you, but don't shove religion down peoples' throats."

"You don't have to take church so seriously, you know."

"You can be a Christian and still 'have fun' on the weekends."

Is that true? Knowing what we do, about the surpassing worth of Christ, is it OK to just do the church thing on Sunday and do my thing the other days of the week? Absolutely not. Following Jesus is an all or nothing deal.

Now, there is a narrow-mindedness that is bad, and it's not what Jesus is referring to in this upcoming passage. Jesus doesn't want us to be arrogant or judgmental of those who are not believers. We stand firm on the truth, while our conduct is saturated with grace. Loving in the truth—the essence of what it means to be a Christian.

But people will still get frustrated with you as you obey God's Word. Opposition will come, and it might not necessarily be because you are arrogant. Jesus said the road that leads to life is narrow. There's no other way to eternal life. That's the truth. And we have to stand firm on our conviction.

There were two verses that I repeatedly came back to as a high school student. These were the words that kept me going when it was hard to live out my faith. Eventually, this passage is what inspired me to encourage you—the next generation—to be uncommon for the sake of the Gospel. Jesus' words in Matthew 7:13-14 should be tattooed in the mind of every young believer.

> *Enter by the narrow gate. For the gate is wide and the way is easy that leads to destruction, and those who enter by it are many. For the gate is narrow and the way is hard that leads to life, and those who find it are few.* —Matthew 7:13-14

I read this passage my sophomore year and realized that in order to be a follower of Jesus, I must be willing to be uncommon—narrow-minded. True significance is found through a gate that is small and on a road that is narrow. The Bible gives us no other options.

Jesus immediately commands us to do what is uncommon. In the four years of high school, you choose from two roads: one that is comfortable and another that is difficult. You can choose to be like everyone else: indulge in temporary pleasures, waste the opportunities of youth, and do what "feels good." Or you can choose to stand out for Christ, accept the ridicule from your peers, and live for the things that will matter 7,000 years from now.

It is not easy to live with an eternal perspective, especially as a teenager. And it is definitely countercultural. But Jesus says the gate that leads to life is narrow. Have you ever been at an airport and tried to go through a turnstile with all of your luggage? It probably didn't work out very well. You can only go through a turnstile one person at a time, holding onto a few belongings—if that. Likewise, we cannot come into God's presence embracing the things of this world.

> *Do not love the world or the things in the world. If anyone loves the world, the love of the Father is not in him. For all that is in the world—the desires of the flesh and the desires of the eyes and pride of life—is not from the Father but is from the world. And the world is passing away along with its desires, but whoever does the will of God abides forever.*
> —1 John 2:15-17

We have to come before Him as we are, humbled, desperate, and completely surrendered to His kingdom cause.

There's no such thing as following Jesus 99.99 percent.

I am sure that you realize that in today's culture, it is not popular to live for Jesus. It is the norm to give up your virginity, and drink your Friday and Saturday nights away. This is what Jesus calls " *... the gate (that) is wide and the way (that) is easy that leads to destruction.*" But

Jesus offers us to something greater than the fleeting pleasures of the world. Through Christ Jesus, we can have supreme worth and purpose (1 Corinthians 6:11). By entering through the narrow gate, God gives us the privilege of being history makers and world changers for His name's sake.

Deciding what path you take is the most important decision you will make in high school. It is going to be a difficult four years, and they're going to fly by. But the narrow road is the path of no regrets. Four years, two roads, and a daily decision about who you are going to live for.

The Challenge

As a brother who wants the best for you in these four years, here is my charge: don't follow the majority. Do not go through high school pursuing your dream college, striving for a 4.0 GPA, dreaming to play college sports, or aspiring to be on homecoming court.

If you want these years to hold eternal significance, you must be willing to take a risk. You must be willing to stand out. You must be willing to take criticism that comes with standing up for your faith. In order to make the most of the years God has given you, you must be willing to be uncommon.

You must make a choice on what your life is going to be about. Not more rules to live by, but a calling to live for.

This book is not about how life gets easier as you follow Christ. I am not promising scholarships, state championships, or even friends. Following Jesus will make high school more difficult. It's a journey countercultural to the world around you. This book is not about how to be a Christian and also be popular. People will call you weird, a Jesus freak, a Bible thumper, too religious, prude—probably all of the above. Some might call you narrow-minded, and in a sense, they are correct. The narrow road is not for those who seek approval from this world. The narrow road is for the few who realize that Jesus and His renown are the only things worth living for. This is a book about how to make the most of your high school experience now, by living for eternity.

Sound interesting?

Priorities, Priorities, Priorities

God gave me some cool opportunities in high school. However, none of my experiences compared to seeing God at work in other students' lives. I saw guys trapped in the snare of pornography transformed into men of integrity. I witnessed girls who sought acceptance from others find their identity in Christ. I saw friends who got wasted on the weekends, embrace the love of Jesus and serve Him in inner-city Detroit. I saw God change lives through the power of His Word. There was no greater satisfaction.

For me, high school is not memorable because of my accomplishments, but because of the way the Holy Spirit moved in my life. By pursuing His kingdom, I had the privilege of partnering with God in His work. Now it is your turn.

The Gospel, and the impact you have on others, are the only things that last. Not only in high school, but also for the rest of your life.

Now, I hope I do not sound like somebody who had it all together.

Beneath all the blessings were also a lot of mistakes. On the journey to live a life of influence, I screwed up more times than I can count. From these mistakes, I learned how to maintain humility, and have faith. But I noticed a common theme in the mistakes that I made. More often than not, my mistakes were because I neglected priorities.

Our lives would be all over the place without priorities. We rely on them to help maintain balance. Priorities are our points of reference when we have to make difficult decisions. If misaligned, priorities can be detrimental, leading us to make dumb decisions.

The five points in this next section, "Make it a Priority," are the stepping-stones to the narrow road. There were many things I wish someone had told me before I got to high school. I want to share these things with you. Some of these lessons, I learned from my own mistakes. Some I learned from the mistakes of others. "Make it a Priority" is also a sneak peak into the rest of the book. Each "priority" offers a taste of the five chapters—the five areas of a high school student's life—that compose the narrow road.

Chapter Two
Make it a Priority: What I Would've Done Differently

Make it a Priority to Get Involved: I wish I had auditioned for the school musical. If I had not grown up doing sports, I'm convinced that my life would have made a phenomenal Disney Channel show.

As much as I love running, there is nothing quite like expressing yourself through song. Spontaneous dance parties and High School Musical impersonations are my specialties—just ask my college roommates.

Every fall, you could find me at our school's fall musical. I am a big fan of theater, and many of my friends were in the productions. The cooperation and organization required to pull off these performances is commendable. No matter what activity we do, we can learn a lot from the perseverance of those involved in the performing arts.

There were two things I did every spring: buy new track spikes and consider auditioning for the spring production. Every spring, I would tell myself I would audition, and every spring, I would fail to follow through. One of my closest friends in high school was heavily involved in our performing arts and would always give me the extra nudge to audition. Practice was scheduled the same time as auditions, so I usually used that as my excuse. But other spring sport athletes had made it work.

In fact, one of the best hurdlers on my team ended up with the star role in the spring musical. If there is one thing I wish I did differently, I totally would have spent one of my spring semesters singing, dancing, and wearing funny clothes.

If your school is fortunate enough to offer the fine arts, don't take it for granted. Tough economic times have forced many schools to cut extracurricular programs. Whether it is going out for the football team, the robotics club, or student council, make it a priority to get involved in high school. It doesn't have to be theater! I just happen to talk about the musical in this instance, because it was an opportunity offered to me that I never took advantage of. And I don't want you to make that mistake! You will always miss 100% of the shots you do not take.

Looking back at high school, you're not going to remember all the specifics, but you will remember the great times you shared while doing what you love. So get involved in something you enjoy! Football, track, and student council were the three activities that occupied much of my time. In each, I made awesome friends and unforgettable memories.

Make it a Priority to Challenge Yourself: I wish I had taken more AP Classes. I was born in Seoul, South Korea. Most Koreans are good at math. Therefore, I should be good at math, but I'm not. So before you start labeling me with the typical Asian stereotypes, let me explain.

I only took two Advanced Placement classes: English Language & Composition and U.S Government and Politics. That is not a lot in the grand scheme of things. In fact, looking back, I would say two should be the bare minimum for high school students. My friends who excelled in their studies took four to five AP classes. At the time, I called them crazy, but now in college, they have received numerous scholarships and are graduating early. No doubt it was a challenge, but your academic success is—more often than not—about your attitude. If you say it's going to suck, then, yes, it will suck. But success starts by tackling challenges with determination.

Pause. I am not saying you need to take every AP class at your school. I'm not that crazy. But here's the thing. If you have a good idea of what you want to study in college, take AP classes that go toward your potential major. For example, if you want to study pre-med, take AP Biology, or if you want to eventually write for a newspaper, take an AP English class. Chances are, you will take those classes when you get to college. But if you pass the AP test in the spring and earn college credit, you can get it out of the way! Not only will you save money, but more importantly, you will save time. Double win.

College classes cost thousands of dollars and take up hundreds of hours of your time. But you can save all that money and time in high school if you make it a priority to challenge yourself academically.

Looking at my freshman year college schedule, I wish I had pushed myself more so I could have gotten some of these annoying required classes out of the way. AP classes might seem intimidating, but remember that the rigor of your schedule is a significant factor colleges look at. Hard works pays off; it's a biblical concept (Proverbs 14:23). Challenge yourself in the classroom. You

do not want to have regrets when applying for college!

Make it a Priority to Have Fun the Right Way: I wish I had not taken dances so seriously. Meet my freshman year crush: Amanda.

Amanda had just transferred to my school and was a cheerleader for my freshman football team. Even though I had never spoken a word to her, I thought it would be a smooth move to ask her to Homecoming. During the week of the dance, I went up to her with a bag of her favorite candy and asked if she would go to the dance with me. Her response? "I'll think about it and get back to you." The worst possible answer you could receive when asking a girl on a date. It's not just a "no," it's a delayed "no." A slow, agonizing "no, you're going to be dateless."

As I walked out to practice that afternoon, some of Amanda's friends came up and told me that she did not want to go with me. They also told me she thought I was weird, but my 15-year-old brain interpreted that as a sign that I still had a shot at dancing with her. Thus, I showed up to Homecoming in a fresh white tuxedo, prepared to pounce at a moment's notice during the first slow dance song. Midway through the night, the music slowed down, my heart sped up, and I knew this was the moment. As I navigated the dance floor searching for Amanda, my 15-year-old heart wasn't prepared for what happened next. Amanda was ready to dance all right. Not with me, but with one of my teammates. She found another date that night, and my hopes for a romantic school dance, like they show on the Disney Channel, were shattered. The back of the cafeteria was my humble abode for the rest of my freshman homecoming dance, as I indulged in free cookies and fruit to soothe the heartache.

It's hilarious to look back at this episode of my life; it's so crazy how seriously I treated a dance! Movies puff up high school dances to seem like something that will affect the rest of your life. Not true. And I'm not just talking about finding a date. When homecoming and prom rolled around, many seemed to think that they had to throw the party of the century. Personally, I don't think one night of mayhem is worth the risk of getting in trouble.

Make it a priority to have fun with the right people. Although the dance wasn't that much fun my freshman year, the after party at my friend Chris' sure made up for it. We sat in his backyard shooting hoops, making s'mores, and attempting ridiculous trick shots with a Frisbee. All while some of our classmates down the street threw a party that eventually got them busted. Trust me, it's possible to have fun without getting drunk or high.

You are only guaranteed four Homecomings and one or two proms in your lifetime—make the most of them! Just some practical advice: unless you have a significant other, riding solo to Homecoming is the way to go. No pressure, you can dance with your friends, and it's easier to form groups for pictures and dinner beforehand. All the mushy-gushy that comes with finding a date tends to create unnecessary drama and tension. The most fun I had at Homecoming was my senior year— the only year I did not ask someone. After getting denied to the dance my freshman year, having a date my sophomore year, and getting denied again as a junior, I found that Homecoming was more fun when you don't hype it up so much!

However, I do recommend you find a date for prom. Whom should you ask? The best date is someone you are already good friends with. Prom is much more couple-friendly than Homecoming. You do not switch dance partners, and will most likely be with your date all night. So make sure you are comfortable with your date! My friend, Liz, was my senior prom date. We were actively involved in our church, so we were used to being around each other. We had also gone on retreats and even served on mission trips in Detroit and Zambia. Because we already had a foundation of a friendship prior to prom, we were comfortable with one other and ended up having a great time. It was just like another night hanging out for us! No awkwardness, no worries, just fun! I could not have asked for a better date for my senior prom. Fellas! Need some ideas on how to ask a girl? Be creative, simple, and sweet! The ladies dig that kind of stuff (I think?)

Many ask me if anything happened between Amanda and me. Despite our awkward beginnings, we became good friends! To make things more initially uncomfortable, we ended up in the same science class my freshman year. Not just in the same class, but in the same lab group! You can imagine how embarrassed I was when our group went to her house to work on a project, and her parents already knew who I was as "sour patch boy". But check this out. Amanda's parents were some of the strongest believers I met in high school. In fact, after sharing our faiths with each other, Amanda's parents sponsored me on every one of my international mission trips. My freshman year crush's parents ended up supporting me so that I could take the Gospel to the ends of the earth. Who would have thought this could all stem from getting denied to homecoming? Indeed, God is sovereign!

Make Purity a Priority: I wish I had not become numb to the value of chastity. Remember in middle school when it was a huge deal to have your first kiss? You were viewed as strange if you didn't kiss someone by the time you got to high school. It doesn't get that much different as you grow up. I know that for me, as a guy, it was tough to value chastity while every other week there seemed to be another rumor about so-and-so hooking up.

At times, I unfortunately became numb to the importance of chastity. I hope you don't make the same mistake. Kissing, making out, etc. was created by God to bring a man and a woman together in physical, emotional, sexual, and spiritual intimacy. That's serious stuff, not something we should ever take lightly.

So why make a big deal out of kissing? I mean, it's only a kiss, right? I'm sure you have that term before; it's "only" a kiss. But "only" a kiss leads to "only" making out, and "only" making out leads to "only" putting your hands where they don't belong, and "only" putting your hands where they don't belong leads to—need I say more? We can't play that game; it's too risky. Sexual temptation is powerful. And once the hormones start raging, we want the next better thing. Thus, when it's not in the right context, sexual temptation leads us down the wide road of regret. Why give the enemy any sort of foothold in our lives, especially in one of the most sensitive areas? That one "innocent kiss" is the beginning of a slippery slope of regret.

I fell down that slope a few times, regrettably. On a few occasions, I believed the lie that "there's nothing wrong with one quick kiss." That turned out to be false. Once you begin to get physically intimate with the opposite sex, you begin to open the gates of your heart. And that's a really good thing, if done in the appropriate context of a marital relationship. My foolish actions resulted in unnecessary heartbreak that I regret. I learned that staying pure isn't only about not having sex until you're married; it's the intimacy you share with someone on all levels physically and emotionally.

One day, I am going to have to sit down with my fiancé and confess all my past sexual sin. I want that conversation to be as least awkward as possible. Mainly because, I want to have the best marriage possible. So why flaunt my purity to people who I will probably lose touch with in a few years?

Here is a statement this generation needs to hear: purity is beautiful. If you are a girl who values your virginity, you shine like a diamond in a crooked and perverse generation. Your chastity is too exquisite to give up to a hormone-raged boy. Don't listen to those who call you "prude" or tell you that you are not having enough fun. The truth is, you are the most beautiful where it counts, in your character and heart. Brothers, we need to protect our sisters' hearts. Their sexual purity is of

utmost value, no doubt, but we must also guard their hearts by being intentional with our actions and words. When you call her at night and ask her out to coffee, she sees that as more than a simple act of friendship. As men, our intentionality is key in respecting those of the opposite sex.

We are all beautiful creations of God. We must not let Satan or the world tell us anything less. Make it a priority to yourself, your future spouse, and to your Heavenly Father to stay pure

for the special person God has planned for you.

Make Fellowship an Utmost Priority: I wish I got involved with my church's high school ministry sooner. It's one thing to *go* to church; it's another thing to *be* the church.

The Bible never references the church as a building. Jesus envisioned His church to be His hands and feet in the world, a force for good known for loving one another (John 13:35). I spent too much of high school going through the motions and simply *going* to church, when Jesus commands us to *be* the church.

It's not that I was struggling in my faith, nor did I have bad feelings toward anyone at my church. I was just incredibly apathetic. I went to Sunday services and youth group on Wednesday, but I was hesitant to get involved. Part of me didn't want to show up alone to youth group; another side of me thought I was fine with just going and listening to the messages. I was a master at finding an excuse not to go to Bible study or sign up for fall retreat. Looking back, I ask myself "What was I thinking?"

It wasn't until I went on my first retreat my junior year, that my eyes were opened to what I was missing out on. For the first time, I experienced fellowship. Not just spending a weekend playing flag football and broomball, but worshipping God together as a body of believers. God opened my eyes to how important it is to surround myself with, and do life with, brothers and sisters in Christ—the church. I had friends at school whom I studied with, and teammates with whom I went to war with on the football field, but until then I didn't have people praying for me, encouraging me, and keeping me accountable in my walk with Christ. "I'm going to know these people 400 years from now," I thought to myself. These fellow believers are my literal brothers and sisters. We share a common bond that can't be broken by Satan or any of his forces. These are the relationships that every high school student must have if they desire to take the narrow road.

Christians have no need to regret, because God makes all things work together for good (Romans 8:28). But if I could change *anything*, it would be this one thing: I wish I had been intentional about fellowship sooner. If I were to do high school over again, I would have gotten involved with my church's high school ministry right off the bat, during freshman year. God used my experiences on retreats, small group parties, and mission trips to inspire me to write this book. Your experiences don't have to result in a book, but one thing is for sure: you're not going grow as a believer without fellowship.

Make fellowship an utmost priority. The people you spend time with have incredible influence on the type of person you become. Take a second to think about your group of friends. Ask yourself, "Are these the type of people that I can call at two in the morning when I'm going through a crisis? Is this someone who won't tell me what I want to hear, but what I need to hear?" Do you have brothers and sisters in your life who are running alongside you on your walk with Christ?

As we talked about in the opening pages, the greatest satisfaction possible in these four years, and for the rest of your life is found in the Kingdom of Heaven. Our goal isn't just to be part of a church gathering on Sundays, but to bring others to a saving knowledge of what we talk about at those Sunday morning gatherings. That's quite a task. And you're going to have a tough time doing it alone. You're going to need people to come alongside you on this journey. For me, my youth group was the means through which I built relationships that helped me in my walk with Christ. Whatever church you attend, I hope that you wouldn't just *go* to that church, but that you will take initiative to *be* the church as Jesus commanded.

Chapter Three
The Narrow Road Through Sports and Extracurriculars

I appeal to you therefore, brothers, by the mercies of God, to present your bodies as a living sacrifice, holy and acceptable to God, which is your spiritual worship.
—Romans 12:1

Living Sacrifices

Although part of me wishes I did the musical, I managed to get involved in several other sports and activities during my high school tenure. Now, this chapter is not meant to be a bragging list of my achievements. Moreover, I want to help you think about what activities you could dive into, if you haven't yet. You see, my goal was never to be successful. My aim was to love and honor my Savior through my gifts, and the same should go for you. Four years will be a drag if all you do is sit in a building for eight hours a day, five days a week, listening to lectures and taking exams. Not to mention waking up at 6 a.m. (looking back, I have no idea how I did it). High school was meant for more than that.

Make the most of your time; get involved. I don't mean

randomly join every club or team at your school. Find the things that interest you and pursue them. At your high school reunion, you are most likely not going to talk to others about the rhetorical analysis you wrote in your English class (of course, there is nothing wrong if you do!). What you will remember are the memories you made while pursuing your passions, which shaped you into the man or woman you're supposed to be. Sports, the arts, clubs, and extracurricular activities are how you discover the niche through which you glorify God. Most try out for the team or the musical for their own recognition; our pursuits are an intentional manner of worship.

Platforms, Platforms, Platforms

When I began to write this chapter, one word came to mind: platforms. You see, our passions and involvements are platforms from which we shine the light of Christ. I used to believe that the only way I could have a platform was if was on ESPN Top Ten Plays. Little did I know, I was chasing something that I had all along. I thought I had to be the starting receiver to have an influence on my teammates. If I didn't get elected class president, part of me doubted that my ministry would be as effective. While professional athletes and celebrities do have powerful influence, the Bible says every follower of Christ plays a role in God's Kingdom mission.

> *You are the light of the world. A city set on a hill cannot be hidden. Nor do people light a lamp and put it under a basket, but on a stand, and it gives light to all in the house. In the same way, let your light shine before others, so that they may see your good works and give glory to your Father who is in heaven.*
> —Matthew 5:14-16

Who were these people Jesus called the "light of the world"? Fishermen, tax collectors, and tradesmen. Not stunning by worldly standards. But guess what? They went on to change the world. Having an influence isn't about being born into the right family or having the best grades; it's about being available to God. No matter who you are or what you do, you have a role to play in the Kingdom of God. We have been hand-placed *by* God, *for* God (Colossians 1:16), to shine his light in a dark world, much like a lighthouse. You don't find lighthouses in valleys or forests. Light must be where it can guide those who are lost, because light shines the brightest in the darkest places.

Jesus says you are that light, and shining is not a suggestion; it's a command. Whatever your platform may be, you are commanded to shine to bring God glory. Whether you play soccer or the clarinet, whether you are president of chess club or DECA, you are a city set on a hill that cannot and should not be hidden.

Even something as simple as your age is a platform. As I wrote this book, most of the reactions I received had to do with my age, not my writing. "You have so many other things to concentrate on at your age," a parent told me. "Twenty-year-olds don't write books!" Exactly. Most don't, but my aim as a follower of Christ has never been to be part of the majority. The narrow road will lead to some decisions the world might see as cuckoo. Trust me, there were many other things I could have done instead of write this book. The transition from high school to college is tough. There were some late nights and tight deadlines. But I realized that God desired to use my age and this stage of life as a platform to share with you, a high school student. I believe that you can better relate to me, simply because I am a few steps ahead of you, more so than if I had decided to wait to work on this project until my forties. And on top of that, this was a passion the Lord gave me when I graduated. So I decided to seize my once-in-a-lifetime platform to shine, and I am praying that you would use whatever you love to do to shine, too.

Free Candy and Pens

I still remember my freshman year orientation. How could I forget after I was besieged by virtually every student organization in my school? Clubs and societies lined up along the walls of the cafeteria, armed with jolly ranchers, in an effort to convince us underclassmen to join their club. I made sure I grabbed as much free stuff as possible; make sure you do the same. Orientation was only the beginning. Throughout the school year, clubs set up tables at lunch or had advertisements on the school news show encouraging you to come out to their meeting. I can't count on two hands the amount of times I have been invited to Spanish Club.

Make sure to check out clubs that spark your interest. If you're interested, attend a meeting or two—it can't hurt! You don't have to commit right away, so why not at least see what they are all about? When searching for ways to get involved, I have two words of advice.

Be Strategic. Four years might seem like a really long time when you are a freshman, but by the time you are a senior, it is hard to believe how quickly four years flew by. Your time is limited. Therefore, be strategic in what you decide to get involved with. Search for clubs and organizations that appeal to your potential college major or career interests. If you are thinking about being a business major, get hooked up with DECA. Enjoy politics? Debate club might be for you. Experience is where you put everything you've learned into practice. For me, an entire semester of learning how to write news stories did not compare to actually being on-air. Class is important. However, experience is how you discover if you truly love doing something.

Maybe you attend a school that does not have a club that sparks your interest. If you're particularly passionate about something, be a leader and make something happen. I had a friend, Haley, who loved to play lacrosse but our school did not have a team. She made some phone calls, talked to friends who were interested, and in 2012, Novi High School women's lacrosse had their inaugural season. Haley was the captain of that team. I love how Haley did not wait for something to happen, but instead took the initiative. Her endeavor is a great example of how we should pursue the things we are passionate about. Colleges and employers love seeing leadership skills and extracurricular involvement on resumes. Being strategic with how you spend your time will give you great opportunities for your future endeavors.

Do What You Love. Often, Christians think that they can only have an influence on others if they are in vocational ministry. Not true. For the believer, there is no such thing as a secular occupation. God doesn't want us to separate our "church" life from our "secular" or "school" life. Following Jesus means that He permeates everything we do. The seismic truth of the Christian faith is that everything that was created exists to glorify God (Colossians 1:16-17). Anything less is a travesty. My third grade teacher once told me to "be the best Derek Kim you can be" and not to be a second-rate version of someone else. So ask yourself, "What am I interested in?" "What issues keep me up at night?" "What is something I can see myself doing for 30 to 40 years?" Whatever it is, find it. Pursue it. Experience it. And use it to expand the kingdom of God.

You see, the moment you decided to follow Jesus, you became a part of the most powerful institution in history: the body of Christ. Ephesians 4 and 1 Corinthians 12 say that all Christians are part of one body functioning for the sole purpose of glorifying Christ. Therefore, it is foolish to think there is only one way to exalt Jesus. Just like a human body; the nose is important, but you can't forget about the eyes. What about the feet that will carry that nose? What about the tendons and ligaments that hold this whole body together? In the Body of Christ, some love to sing and dance, and others enjoy teaching French, while several get excited about fighting global injustice. High school is the time to discover, develop, and display your individual interests and gifts for His glory.

Our society does a fantastic job of encouraging all the right things for all the wrong reasons. Specifically, for your sake, I'm talking about getting into college. Yes, going to college should be the endeavor of every 15-to 18-year-old. But a more worthy goal is to discover your talents and passions in an effort to offer our bodies as living sacrifices, as the opening verse of this chapter states.

So don't join a club just to build up your resume. Don't try out for the team simply because everyone else is doing it. Do what you love. When you delight yourself in the Lord, everything else falls into place (Psalm 37:4). He promises to be faithful; your job is to pursue Him in every endeavor (Matthew 6:33; Proverbs 16:3).

The Christian Athlete

Shout out to all the competitors out there! Sports have taught me lessons like hard work and perseverance in ways that are just not possible in a classroom. I definitely have a special place in my heart for competition, but have you ever thought about what it means to be a Christian athlete? Practically, as high school students, what does it look like to glorify God through your sport?

During a game against Plymouth my senior year, a cornerback heckled me about the Bible verses that were written on my shoes. I am not going to repeat the words that were exchanged, but he implied that I was "soft" because I was a Christian. Sure, I wasn't the best blocker on the team, but really? Christians are known for being "soft"? Unfortunately, I think this is a common misconception. Many people have this image of Jesus from pictures they've seen, as a bearded man who holds children on His lap and sheep on His shoulders. Yes, there is a gentle, caring side to Jesus. But Christ is also an all-powerful, all-knowing, all-seeing Savior who is coming again on a white horse to defeat Satan and restore order to the universe.

Right now, as you read, and even before you were born, angels have never ceased singing *"Holy, holy, holy, is the Lord God almighty, who was and is and is to come!"* God is so holy, so set apart, so perfectly unique, that when He came down from heaven to Mt. Sinai to deliver the Torah, no one could touch the mountain and live (Exodus 19). No words can begin to express His infinite worth. Jesus is infinitely worthy *"to receive power and wealth and wisdom and might and honor and glory and blessing!"* (Revelation 5:12). And guess what? This holy, perfect God was spit on, whipped, and died on a tree to give us life—that is anything but "soft"! He is your motivation every time you step on the track, jump into the pool, or run onto the field.

Thus, the Christian athlete is the most intense athlete.

For the Christian, the audience is not the fans in the stands, coaches, teammates, or college recruiters.

Christians compete for an audience of one. (AO1) When I began competing on the national level, pride swelled up inside of me. My thoughts were increasingly centered on my accomplishments, not God's faithfulness. It wasn't that I was going around bragging about my performance. I still prayed and read my Bible before I ran. I even tried to share my faith at meets. But the pressure to perform well made it more of a challenge to delight in God through my running.

Admit it, there's a part of us that craves recognition. It's a bit easier to run faster or jump higher when there are hundreds of people watching of if there is a cute girl in the stands. The problem with this is that our joy becomes confined to the words of your coaches, teammates, and fans. When we perform horribly, we feel horribly. Your coach cusses you out, and you actually start to believe what he says.

Worst of all, we rob God of the glory only He deserves.

For freedom Christ has set us free; stand firm therefore,
and do not submit again to a yoke of slavery.
—Galatians 5:1

Do you sense a hint of irony in Paul's statement? It's almost like he is saying, "Dude, in Christ you're free, so why do you keep doing things that enslave you?" Very loose translation, I know. But do you see what I am saying? In Christ, we are free from sin, hell, our past, a wasted life—and for the sake of this conversation—the opinions of others. You no longer need to be motivated by fear of failure, because you have experienced perfect love. Christ frees you to compete to your full potential.

It's a popular coaching cliché to say, "True character is what you do when no one is watching." For the Christian athlete, however, there is always an audience—an audience of one. Jesus is our coach. Jesus is our fan base. Jesus is the reason we compete. Whether it's a 6 a.m. weightlifting session, or the state championship game, God deserves glory through your attitude and effort.

Every time you step onto that field, tell yourself, "Jesus is my audience, and His opinion is the only one that matters." Even if you drop the baton or can't finish the set, He still loves you. His love is unconditional. Isn't that so freeing and motivating? You don't have to be a part of the starting lineup, or break the school record, to receive His love. If you are a follower of Christ, God is fully satisfied with you. He loves you eternally and perfectly not because of what you have done, but because of Jesus' life, death, resurrection, and Spirit who now dwells in you. The Christian does not compete *for* God, but *with* God, and thus, no one can steal a Christian athlete's joy.

Hard Work is Biblical. Playing for an audience of one does not mean we are content with second place. The Christian athlete is the hardest worker on the team. Be the first one in the gym and the last one to leave. Never cuts corners and always put in extra reps. Live in the weight room. Outwork your opponent on and off the field. Not to be a suck-up, but because you have been saved by grace, and are eternally grateful. Our sports are now a mechanism through which we worship God, a living, breathing thank you note.

> *Whatever you do, work heartily, as for the Lord and not*
> *for men.*
> —Colossians 3:23

Working hard is not something your coach made up. Hard work is a biblical concept. The book of Proverbs is filled with commandments to toil for the LORD. Here is one I write on my hand before every practice:

> *In all toil there is profit, but mere talk tends only to*
> *poverty.*
> —Proverbs 14:23

It's so easy to talk, isn't it? Whenever I would drop a pass or run a slow race, I was tempted to bring up past accomplishments or make excuses. It's one thing to say we will finish the workout, but it's another thing to actually do it.

The Bible says, "Shut up, Derek, and work" (there goes my loose Bible translation yet again). God doesn't like empty talk anymore than you do. There's no point in boasting of something you don't have. As Christians, we are charged to work our butts off for the Lord. He promises that hard work—in some way, shape, or form—always pays off (Colossians 3:23-24). Isn't that an awesome promise in a world where coaches can be unfair and political, and favoritism often determines playing time? The profit might not come until down the road. Like on your first job, when you have to work the 6 a.m. shift. But after waking up for morning practice five times a week, a morning work shift is a piece of cake. You'll probably never forget the agony of bench press burnouts. Good thing it taught you how to persevere through finals in your freshman year of college. Your blood, sweat, and tears might not result in a college scholarship. But God is faithful. He knows what He is doing. Our job is to put in the work and trust Him.

There was a point in my sophomore year where I became the definition of a gym rat. I practically lived in the weight room, and protein powder was my best friend. Coaches had to kick me out at times because I refused to leave. I told myself that others might be naturally bigger, stronger, or faster; but no one would ever outwork me. During stadium stairs, I made sure I was ahead of others who played my position. If we were running 300s at track practice, I made an effort to finish each rep faster than the last one. There were cramps, and a lot of time spent puking into a trashcan, but I never once regretted working hard.

Extra work is great, but working hard doesn't necessarily mean working longer; it's about working smarter. Don't just go through the motions. Every repetition counts. Instead of making it your goal to be in the weight room for a certain amount of time, aim to complete every task with 110% effort. Punish every repetition and set. Be the hammer, not the nail. You'll get more out of an hour-long lift giving total effort rather than three hours of loitering in the weight room. This way, you toil for the Lord while also saving time. Double-win.

Dignity of Christ. Competing hard doesn't mean being a jerk to your opponents or teammates.

Following work ethic, the way you carry yourself on the field speaks to what is written on your heart. As an athlete, you have a powerful platform. The world loves sports, and high school athletics are no exception. When you throw on that jersey, you represent a family, school, community, and a risen Savior who rules the Milky Way. Therefore, we need to watch the words we whisper under our breath when conditioning gets tougher than the week before. You represent much more than yourself when you compete. Remember that. As James said, we must be *"quick to hear, slow to speak, slow to anger"* (James 1:19).

> The eyes of the LORD are in every place, keeping watch
> on the evil and the good.
> —Proverbs 15:3

Is the way you talk in the locker room pleasing in God's eyes? When an opponent cheap shots you, do you respond in Christ-like humility? Christian athletes display the dignity of Christ through every word and deed. They submit to their coaches and team managers because to dishonor them is to dishonor the One who put them there (Romans 13:1-2). Christian athletes should go out of their way to encourage teammates. The season can get long, and coaches scold you 100 times before they compliment you once. Breathe life into your teammates through words of encouragement.

You never know how uplifting your words could be. I'll never forget when the varsity players gave me recognition for being the only sophomore at the 6 a.m. lifting sessions. Imagine how pathetic a lanky wide receiver looked in a room of junior and senior offensive linemen (not to mention I was basically asleep between sets). One of the best ways to encourage is to avoid showing favoritism. Whether it is the team captain, or the third-string punter, every teammate matters to God. Therefore, they should matter to us. God warns us in James 2:1-13 to avoid the sin of partiality. Imagine if God had favorites. Chances are you wouldn't be a starter. Thankfully, His grace applies to all. We need to see people, like God sees people. This doesn't mean you have to be best friends with all of your teammates. You're going to have close friends whom you tend to get along well with. But would you be cool with

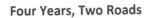

standing next to a different group of girls in the formation? Do you treat the backups the same way you treat the starters? Your coaches probably won't. So be the teammate who makes practice a bit more tolerable. We're not suck-ups—every team has enough of those. We are images of the grace and truth that has changed our lives.

NARPS Unite

Shout out to all the non-athletic regular people (NARPS) out there! I understand that sports aren't for everyone, and you know what? That's totally cool. However, this doesn't mean that you do not have a platform that you can use to glorify God! There are still plenty of reasons to get involved during this short four year period known as high school, whether it is debate club or by getting a job. And never forget, there is always the school musical!

Even though you might not have an 80 mph fastball like some of your peers, any activity allows you to meet people outside your group of friends. This is invaluable. Learning to interact with different people is an essential life skill; you're going to be doing it for the rest of your life. No matter how old you get, you will be drawn to people who are similar to you. It's time to break out of the mold; high school is great time to develop the habit of going out of your comfort zone. The dude you're on yearbook staff with is probably not the type of person you would chill with on a Friday night, and that's cool. But when you strive toward a goal with others—different types of characters—you learn to love people and work with others who are different than you. It's what the Christian life is all about. Imagine how different the Bible would be if Jesus, Paul, and the Twelve Disciples didn't break out of society's norms. You wouldn't have the amazing story we have today, that's for sure. Look at Jesus' example.

> *And as Jesus reclined at the table in the house, behold, many tax collectors and sinners came and were reclining with Jesus and his disciples. And when the Pharisees saw this, they said to his disciples, "Why does*

your teacher eat with tax collectors and sinners?"
—Matthew 9:10-11

There never has, nor will ever be, a greater example of someone who truly loved people.

While the hypocritical Pharisees scoffed at the thought of associating themselves with those of different reputations, the Son of God sat down and ate with the prostitutes, tax collectors, and sinners. Jesus loved them not *in spite* of their differences, but *because* of their differences. I hope that you will decide to be Jesus to your student body. It doesn't matter how others view your club. Your affiliation with those individuals is your opportunity to love out loud. People might think it's weird that you're a part of "that crowd," but who cares? Normal is overrated anyways. Not sure about where to get started? Here are some suggestions.

- **Get a Job!** What a great way to learn responsibilities such as timeliness, managing money, and working under pressure. It's never too early to save for college, and a little spending money doesn't hurt either.
- **Yearbook Staff!** Someone has to assemble that hodgepodge of memories. You creative types will enjoy putting together a project that will be cherished for years to come. Calling all writers, photographers, and designers!
- **Student Council!** Through student government, you get to plan school events, be a voice for your classmates, and learn leadership skills. Your school is a democracy; who's going to lead the charge?
- **Be an Athletic Team Manager!** Do you love sports, but don't exactly boast the 30 plus-inch vertical? Talk to a coach, and see if he or she could use some help during the season. You can still contribute to a team's success without ever putting on a uniform!
- **THE MUSICAL!** Do we have to go over this again?

Hold up! I'm not done yet!

I couldn't just give the athletes a three-part exhortation, and leave my non-athletic brothers and sisters with a single point!

Regardless of the nature of your involvement, time management is perhaps one of the most practical life skills you could learn. As you progress through your high school years, you'll be shocked at how fast it goes. Don't blink, freshman. You will be a senior before you know it. Your time is limited; all the more reason why you must learn to plan ahead.

Writing stuff down is a good place to start. In your planner, use both the monthly and weekly calendars. Here's what I did: My monthly schedule was comprised of my definite activities such as church events, athletic competitions, and exams. These were things that were pretty clear-cut and unavoidable. I would then prioritize and prepare for these events accordingly. Then, there was my weekly schedule, where I foresaw the upcoming week's appointments, such as homework, working out, or meeting a friend at a coffee shop. This was stuff that was important, but not absolute. That flexibility was necessary because a crucial component of time management is learning how to say "no." Allow yourself grace when you plan. You only have so much time in the week. It's just not realistic to accomplish everything you would "like" to do. This is not an excuse to be a lazy; it's allowing yourself to be a human being. Life is crazy, stuff comes up, and we must be prepared to readjust. And, if you don't manage your schedule, your schedule will manage you.

What is Leadership?

It begins during your first days of school. You're told to "be a leader" through your words and actions. Whether it is group projects, committees, or bands, it doesn't seem to be enough just to be on the team. Colleges and parents urge leadership. It's even reflected in the corporate world. Every championship team has veteran players who are leaders, and successful corporations have capable CEOs. Let me start off by saying that it's great that leadership is valued in society. Leadership is a noble task, however, the word is tossed around so much that its true meaning is often forgotten.

> *...But whoever would be great among you must be your servant, and whoever would be first among you must be your slave, even as the Son of Man came not to be served but to serve, and to give his life as a ransom for many.*
> —Matthew 20:26-28

Leaders are servants. The least are the greatest. The first are last, and the last are first. Here comes Jesus once again to flip the world's ideals on its head. He says that the race to the top is a sprint toward humility. To Him, it's not about having the highest GPA, fastest mile split, or the most volunteer hours. Jesus is looking for leaders who will serve, because serving and leading are synonymous in His book. This theme is all throughout Scripture, notably in Philippians 2:1-11. Paul speaks in astonishment of how Jesus did not seize His equal position with God. Instead, He continued to empty Himself for the sake of grace. If Jesus—the greatest leader of all time—led through humility, that says something about how we should lead.

Wouldn't you want to follow a leader like Jesus? I would much rather be on a team fueled by servitude rather than one led by a sense of entitlement. This was precisely my aim when I ran for student government. Now, trust me, I wasn't the perfect class president. There were a few years where homecoming decorations were sub-par and school spirit dwindled. Nonetheless, my overall goal was to represent my classmates through Christ-like humility.

During my years in office, I was reelected against candidates who were more popular, smarter, and frankly, more deserving. These guys were tremendously respected in my school. Today, they are division one athletes, fraternity presidents, and the kind of people who make their parents proud. But there was one big difference among our campaign mantras. While they tried to win our classmates' respect with promises of what they would do, I sought to earn their respect through a sense of gratitude. I didn't talk about "why" they should vote for me. Instead, I shared how it would be a privilege for me to represent them as my friends. My speech was filled with my willingness to serve, rather than my laundry list of accomplishments.

It worked out pretty well.

Just think about when someone puts your needs before theirs. It's not a burden to follow someone like that. Humility goes a long way in a world that is obsessed with entitlement. The human heart reacts well to servitude, and it is my prayer that you would be a leader who exhibits the meekness of Christ.

Nowhere have I seen servant leadership better exhibited than through my friend, Kirk Cousins. As a record-breaking quarterback at Michigan State, Kirk has a lot to brag about. He was voted captain as a sophomore, and led the Spartans to their first Big Ten championship in twenty years—just to name a couple of his accomplishments. But, above all, people know Kirk as a servant. He was more concerned about taking his team to the Rose Bowl than breaking individual quarterback records. He would go out of his way to invite other student-athletes to Bible Study rather than gravitating only toward the football squad. When a fan asked for a picture or autograph, Kirk would always introduce himself and ask for their name in return. Kirk was well respected on and off the field during his tenure in East Lansing. And because of his humility, he is remembered for much more than football.

As you strive to get involved, be a leader. Teams and organizations cannot be successful without them. More so, yearn to be the kind of leader Jesus was. Anyone can give orders and boss people around. But it takes a special kind of person to earn the respect of his or her followers. This kind of leadership is rare, but it is the only kind of leadership found in the Kingdom of Heaven.

"Ohana" Means…

Family! Thank you my fellow Lilo & Stitch fans!
You will benefit by getting involved. High school—much like

many things in life—is what you make of it. But as fun as it is to be involved, don't neglect the more important things, namely, family.

Once I found my niche, I was scarcely around the house. With classes during the day, and practice after school, by the time I was back home, I either had to jet to youth group or study for an exam. Unfortunately, more often than not, family time took a backseat.

It only got worse as I got older. I might as well have called myself a "nomad" during the summer before heading off to college. I'd be out with my friends from sunrise to sunset, grabbing a bite to eat, hanging out at the lake, a bonfire, and making all the memories we could before we all went to our respective universities. Meanwhile, my parents would call me from the dinner table every night, asking if I was going to join them. Regrettably, I rarely would. My aim was to spend as much time with my friends as possible because I would miss them once classes started.

But, little did I know, my relationship with my parents would be what I would miss the most.

This hit me hard once I got to East Lansing. After a long morning of setting up my 11X12 feet dorm, which would be my home for the next eight months, my mom and dad took off. It was the beginning of my young adult life. Tears streamed down my face as soon as the elevator took them downstairs. It was all hitting me: my dad wouldn't be praying for me beside my bed at 5 a.m., my mom's *bokumbab* wouldn't be my lunch of choice every Saturday, and laundry was now my responsibility. I barreled down six flights of stairs and chased my parents' car just before they pulled out. On the passenger side of their GMC Acadia, I sobbed, apologizing for not spending more time with them in the past months. At that moment, I didn't care about bonfires, drive-in movies, or anything else I did with my buddies that past summer. Family time was what I was going to miss the most.

Family is an impenetrable bond—the first institution God established when he created the earth (Genesis 2:18-25). It's a weird thought, but the friends you have now might not be there, ten, even two years from now. But guess what? Family will always be family. Your brother isn't going to stop being your brother when you graduate college.

The woman who brought you into this world will be your mom even after you get married.

Work your butt off to get a starting spot next season, toil to ensure your campaign for class secretary is successful, but never forget how much your parents have sacrificed for you. If it weren't for their dedication, you wouldn't have even made it this far. Most students can't wait to move out of the house so they can be independent. That is what most people do, the wide road. But the narrow road is found in honoring your parents, which is the key to a long, prosperous life (Exodus 20:12).

The sacrificial love of your parents is a reflection of Jesus's sacrifice for our souls. Why did Jesus die on the cross while we were still His enemies? Because He loved us and wanted to give us the opportunity to know Him (Romans 5:8). Why do your parents—day in and day out—clothe you, feed you, and pay for your cell phone bill? Because they love you and seek to set you up for your future.

Some of you have already tuned me out. Sounds like an encore of the argument you had with your mom last night. From firsthand experience, I know that tension builds up in the house as you get older. You might be long awaiting the day you have independence to make your own decisions. That day will come in its time. Meanwhile, know that if your life was endangered, your parents would give their life for you, no questions asked (ask them). It was when I got to college that I realized my mom and dad did all those things—calling me on Friday nights asking when I was coming home, pushing me in my studies, yelling at me to go to bed early—because they wanted the best for me. My prayer is that it wouldn't take you as long as it took me to realize the blessing our parents are.

Now, some of you may say, "It's their job to feed me and pay for my dental insurance." But they really don't *have* to do all those things; it's no benefit to them. Your mom doesn't profit from encouraging good study habits. Your dad doesn't get anything out of working eight hours a day, five days a week to buy the clothes on your back. Their toil is a sacrifice of their money and time. Could there be better evidence of their love for you? When your mom and dad keep nagging you about college applications, it is because they want you to make the most of your opportunities. If they just let you waste your blessings, what kind of parents would they be? Not very good ones.

This kind of love is not normal. I know that it is so cliché to say that "Your parents love you." But really wanting the best for someone? That's not natural. That involves sacrificing part of yourself without getting anything in return. It is finding joy in someone else's well being. This love is not normal; this love is supernatural, and this is the love your mom and dad have always had for you.

Learn to communicate with your parents. Just like any other human being, they have things that make them mad, questions that are hard to answer. Be open with them. If they said something to you that hurt, gently let them know (Proverbs 15:1). Likewise, if you sense that something you said offended them, show humility and apologize. Newsflash: your parents aren't perfect, and neither are you. Communicate, forgive, and move on. They are going to make mistakes; much like you and I do every day.

If I could go back in time, I would have been more intentional about spending time with my family. An easy way to do this is by prioritizing dinnertime. Amidst the craziness of your schedule, be intentional about having dinner with your family. Let Mom and Dad know how school is going. Ask your siblings how soccer practice went. Spend some time shooting hoops with your dad when he rolls into the driveway. Life is only going to get busier. Why not set aside a daily chunk of your life to be with those who love you the most?

Your parents will have spent about $300,000 on you by the time you are 17 years old[iii]. That's enough money to buy a lot of Lamborghinis or plane tickets to Europe. Take a second to thank your parents and tell them you love them. The house you live in, the education you are getting, and even your physical wellness would not be possible without your parents' sacrifice. Then, reflect on Jesus's sacrifice that enabled you to have eternal life. Endless joy, a peace that transcends all understanding, and true hope would not be possible without His sacrifice.

A Special Shout Out.

It'd be foolish of me to assume all of you come from perfect households. Broken families are on the rise all around the world. Some of you might live with an aunt, uncle, or grandparent. Maybe you've never known your mom or dad, or have lost one of them.

I have no right to say I know how you feel; I don't, and I hope I do not sound like I do. What I do know, however, is that God calls us to honor our parents. The commandment to honor our parents is allegorical of a higher calling: a call to honor our Heavenly Father, the supreme authority of time and space. This applies to everybody, no matter what you have been through. You don't come from a "normal" household? That is all right. You have that much more of a platform to honor God and whomever else He has put as an authority in your life. Remember when we agreed that light shines the brightest in the darkest places? God can—and wants to be—the father you never had. He's waiting with open arms. That can be a difficult process. But God has placed brothers and sisters within the Body of Christ to encourage you, some whom He will use as a father or mother figure in your life. Keep an eye out for them. Maybe it's a pastor, a small group leader, a coach, a teacher, counselor, or someone who lives in your neighborhood. Unlike our earthly fathers, our Heavenly Father is perfect. No matter what you have been through, we can rest in knowing that God, as a loving Father, will never leave us or forsake us.

Good

I know there is a lot of pressure to be successful. Coaches want to win, and college admissions demand a lot from their applicants. Extra stress from parents sure doesn't lighten the load. That being said, we must never lose sight of God's faithfulness.

You may be thinking, "How does God's faithfulness tie in with my involvement?" Well, look at it this way. As long as you are following Christ and honoring Him in whatever you do, God will use your story for His glory.

You can't lose, Christian.

And we know that for those who love God all things work together for good, for those who are called according to his purpose. For those whom he foreknew

he also predestined to be conformed to the image of his Son, in order that he might be the firstborn among many brothers.
—Romans 8:28

How freeing!

We can rest in the assurance that God is bigger than our successes and failures. You didn't make the varsity team, or first chair clarinet. Soccer season didn't go so well, or your dance competition was sub-par this weekend; it's okay. God is in control. He has a plan for your circumstance. Our job is to be faithful with what He has called us to do right here, right now, by honoring Him in our efforts and attitudes. Our ultimate prize is in Heaven, but sometimes, God, out of His mercy, rewards us here on earth, as well.

Before heading to the state finals to wrap up my junior track season, I had broken school records in two events. In the process, I had also qualified for the national meet, which would be an awesome opportunity to gain exposure for running at the next level. On a hot, muggy day in June, with sweat across my brow and the "Novi" name printed on my chest, I stepped into the starting blocks at Rockford High School, 110 meters and 10 hurdles away from All-State accolades and a possible state title. As the gun popped, the crowd roared. I could hear the encouragement of my teammates and the screams of my coaches. "Drive!" "Keep your hips up!" "Snap your lead leg!" The first half of my race had gotten off to a great start. Right in the middle of the pack, I strained to bring together all that I had practiced the past few months, as I inched meters closer to Michigan high school track and field glory.

Then, it happened.

On the ninth hurdle, 15 meters away from the finish line, my trail leg caught the ricochet of the hurdle in lane four. Next thing I knew, I was lying on the track—facedown—with all my hopes of a state title crushed. I knew that my disqualification marred my chances of running in college. No Division One coach was going to recruit an athlete who didn't score at the state finals.

Thankfully, I still had one more shot.

My success earlier in the season gave me one more chance to make a name for myself, at the New Balance Outdoor Nationals in Greensboro, North Carolina. Although I did not have high expectations, my coach told me that I had a shot at placing in the shuttle hurdles—and that's exactly what happened. Two weeks after my regrettable tumble, our shuttle hurdle relay took fifth place at the national level, which qualified us for All-American status. I'll never forget the jubilee of crossing the finish line, knowing that I had just made history. Once I got back to Michigan, the college recruiting letters began to pile in. My dream of running at the next level was revived, not by my athleticism, but through the promise of Romans 8:28. Even though I didn't have a state title like most of the people at that meet, I had confidence in God's faithfulness; He used my lame situation for good. He has a good habit of doing that. Remember the cross? There's no greater example of God's faithfulness. Lame is a less than appropriate word to describe God's Son hanging on a cross. But what about now? What is the cross known for? The horrific method of Roman torture is now the greatest example of grace. God wants to make your mess His message. The question is, do you trust Him?

Look, high school can be tough. All the involvement can be draining. Naturally, you're going to have some disappointments. But never forget the freedom that you have in Jesus. You don't have to worry about failure. As long as your utmost pursuit is the glorification of Christ, you can't lose. You're going to lose some games, and events won't always go smoothly. But God is faithful. He will never stop being who He is. He is sovereign over every hair on your head; not a drop of rain falls to the earth unless He allows it to. Everyone loves to say, "Everything happens for a reason." That statement doesn't make sense if there isn't a sovereign God who cares about our lives. Have you ever thought about what that "reason" is? For the Christian, the one who loves Jesus, that reason is "good." All things work together for good. Jesus is that definition of "good." Compete hard. Perform passionately. Build relationships. Spend time with your family. But never forget the One you do it for, the One who makes all things work together for good.

Chapter Four
Year One: Freshman Year

Let no one despise you for your youth, but set the believers
an example in speech, in conduct, in love, in faith, in purity.
—1 Timothy 4:12

Welcome to high school, freshman!

You have a highly influential platform this year. Yes, you heard me correctly. Sure, the upperclassmen may not look up to your 5'2 frame, but youth has always been a powerful pedestal of influence, even in Biblical times.

Perhaps you've stumbled across Paul's letters to Timothy while flipping through the New Testament. You want to talk about a guy who had to beat the odds? Let's talk about Timothy. To start off, his father was a Greek, which means he did not spiritually invest into his life. Scholars also believe that he died before Timothy met Paul. Thus, Timothy was raised by his mother and grandmother, who both taught him the Scriptures (2 Timothy 3:15). On top of everything, Greek culture looked down on someone like a half Hebrew, half Greek, Timothy, since he was raised by two women in a male-dominated society.

Despite this, the Apostle Paul meets Timothy on his first

missionary journey. Not only so, but Paul leads him to Christ and quickly becomes a father-like figure to him (Acts 1:2 and 18). The young apostle goes from Greek culture reject to a world-changer for the Gospel. Timothy, being somewhere in his thirties, was young for being in vocational ministry. We know, from the words of Paul, that the young apostle was often looked down upon because of his youth. It's easy to get discouraged when others doubt you. But Paul exhorts Timothy that his youth is his God-given platform to preach the Gospel.

This pattern is seen in the Old Testament as well. Take King Josiah, for example. I don't know what you did when you were eight years old. I, for one, was still learning how to tie my shoes. Josiah, he became the king of Judah. Whoa. Not only was he an eight-year-old king, but Josiah brought God's people back to the exclusive worship of Yahweh, destroying all other forms of false worship that were being practiced in the day (2 Kings 22 and 23). God did not see Josiah's youth as a disadvantage. Much like Timothy, Josiah's age was a platform from which God was able to display His faithfulness. The same can be true for you.

Young people have exemplary influence. Just look at the sports world. What's so fascinating about athletes like LeBron James, Bryce Harper, and Maria Sharapova? They accomplished great feats that are uncommon at their age. Four MVP awards, a major league contract, and winning the Wimbledon aren't frequent accomplishments for those in their twenties. Age is what made their achievements so special. It was their ultimate platform, and it's yours as well.

While I was writing this book, a common compliment I got was how uncommon it is to be a 20-year-old author. Exactly. *We aren't called to be common*. On the narrow road, we do things that don't fit the norm. In the Kingdom of Heaven, our weakness is the platform upon which God displays His power (2 Corinthians 12:9-10). All you need to do is to be available.

Word travels fast through your school. Gossip is unfortunately a good example of that. However, positive news can permeate hallway chatter as well. You may feel like a nobody in a lunchroom of hundreds of classmates, but more people know who you are than you think. In other words, people are observing your life. And if you're a freshman, everyone knows you're a freshman. It may be because of your short stature and bright green braces, but, nevertheless, the point remains. You have an influence, and it would be a waste not to take advantage of it. Why wait until you're an upperclassman to be unashamed for Christ when you can have an impact today? How you spend your weekends, the words that come out of your mouth, and the way you treat teachers and classmates, all speak truth to what you stand for. It's awesome to see juniors or seniors lead Bible studies and go on mission trips, but how powerful would it be to for upperclassmen to see maturity and a love for the Bible in a 15-year-old? Not much is expected of you as a freshman; thus, there is all the more room for God to glorify Himself.

Before Paul died, his last words were penned to his beloved child in the faith—Timothy. In his first letter (1 Timothy), Paul addressed doctrine and church matters. In his second letter, he makes one last plea to Timothy. Paul's exhortation is the same that I give to you: live unashamed for Christ (1:8), gladly accept persecution for Christ (2:3), pursue the good things of God (2:22), and fight the good fight (4:7).

Don't let anyone look down on you because of your age. *You* set the example for others to follow. Don't waste your influence this year.

Chapter Five
The Narrow Road Through Academics

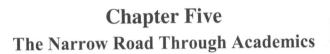

...Everyone to whom much was given, of him much will be required, and from him to whom they entrusted much, they will demand the more.
—Luke 12:48

A wise man is full of strength, and a man of knowledge enhances his might.
—Proverbs 24:5

Find Your Sound and Play it Loud

I want to sincerely thank those of you who decided not to skip this chapter. I contemplated whether to include this part because I know the last thing you want to hear is another person telling you to study. I also understand talking about school is not the most exciting topic. My aim isn't to teach you the quadratic formula or how to write a book report. My focus in this chapter is to help you realize the blessing at your disposal: an education. In high school, you begin to discover your gifts, develop them, and learn how to use them to change the world.

My middle school band director had a saying he used to help

students select an instrument: *find your sound and play it loud.* His words have value for band geeks and non-band geeks alike. Find what you love to do, and play it loud and proud.

Even though I wasn't the most talented clarinet player, I did look forward to our recitals. I loved how each instrument, from the banging bass drum to the elegant flute, played a role in creating a magnificent sound. Much like the instruments of a band, God's children each have a part to play in His orchestra of redemption. He has fearfully and wonderfully crafted each of us with a particular sound to play. Discovering and using our sound is our response to God's grace, a thank-you-letter for all He has done for us. For some of us it will be teaching in the inner city, for others it will be finding a cure for cancer, maybe for you, it's being a voice for justice as a lawyer. Whether it is journalism or finance, whether it is architecture or the oboe, whether it is French or art history, find your sound and play it loud. Discover what you love, develop your passion, and use it to be a difference maker for Christ.

Thank You, Nixon

Have your parents ever answered you complaints with, "*Be thankful because there are starving children in Africa*"? The veracity behind such statements is tragically overlooked. While I would rather not quote a dictator, Joseph Stalin offered a demoralizing, yet insightful thought when he said, "*The death of one man is a tragedy. The death of millions is a statistic.*" Sadly, in our wealthy culture, it's easy to become numb to statistics. As followers of Jesus Christ, we must fight the temptation of letting God's children become merely a number.

Millions of children around the world today have dreams just like us, dreams to be student-athletes, doctors, and lawyers. However, their dreams have a slim chance of becoming reality because their access to education is limited. I have been fortunate to meet some of the faces that make up this statistic. I want you to meet my friend who lives in a village outside of Lusaka, Zambia. You might complain about your second hour class today; he won't. When you finally put a face to a statistic, you realize you have nothing to complain about.

This is Nixon. We met during the last day of my mission trip to Zambia. Nixon wants to be a businessman when he grows up. He enjoys mathematics, soccer, and wants to start a family one day. He lives in a hut with his parents, two brothers, and sister. His mom and dad spend their week selling fruits and vegetables so they can afford to send Nixon to school. Thus, Nixon barely gets to see his parents. Not to mention he walks five miles every morning just to get to his school. The perseverance and sacrifice of Nixon's parents is a testament to the value of education. To them, going to school is more than a matter of waking

up early and writing essays; it is the groundwork upon which Nixon will build his future. At the end of our time together, Nixon told me I had been an encouragement to him. I prayed with my new friend, gave him a hug, and handed him a piece of paper with this verse on it.

The heart of him who has understanding seeks knowledge, but the mouths of fools feed on folly.
—Proverbs 15:14

Little did Nixon know, that he had been a far greater encouragement to me, than I to him.

In America, we have access to public education, which is free and provides everything from textbooks to transportation. It is not like that everywhere in the world.

Here are some numbers for you from Richard Stearn's book *The Hole in Our Gospel.*

- The United States spends approximately $1,780 per capita on primary and secondary education; Uganda spends $5 per capita.[iv]
- Today, one in six adults globally cannot read or write,

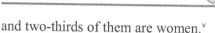
and two-thirds of them are women.[v]

- There are more slaves today than at all other times in history combined. Out of the estimated 27 million in bondage, half of them are children.[vi]

Access to education is a narrow gate in and of itself. It is not a right, but a privilege to wake up and have the opportunity to learn. Living in America, we are part of a significant global minority. Kids like Nixon are real people; they are students with likes and dislikes just like us. The only difference between them and us is latitude and longitude.

This is not a guilt trip; this is reality.

If you are able to read this sentence, you have a stewardship to God and to our brothers and sisters across the globe. We should not be foolish and fail to make the most of our education. As those who walk along the narrow road, we have a responsibility to seize our aptitudes and develop them for God's Kingdom.

The Drag

No subject did I despise more than mathematics.

Maybe some of you can relate. No disrespect to any of my teachers. In fact, Mrs. Thomson, my geometry and algebra teacher, was one of the best instructors I ever had. Math is just something I don't have a passion for, and I am okay with that. There are some things we don't particularly enjoy doing, no matter how many times we do them. And trigonometry is not the only thing that can plague the high school experience.

As I trekked through the latter half of high school, I experienced what I call "the drag." "Drag" is how you feel as an upperclassman who is ready to be done. With summer on the horizon, school was just a nuisance. All that was on my mind was prom, track season, senior all-night party, and the last day of school.

However, between me and my diploma lay a cornucopia of assignments, papers, and exams. There are classes you won't enjoy in high school. You will face "the drag." But your attitude and mindset will determine how you get through it. I remember times I would wake up with a pessimistic attitude on my way to school and literally drag myself to class. There were times when I would sit down to write a paper and think only about how much I didn't want to do it. No doubt, my cynicism made the task at hand much more loathsome than it had to be.

It doesn't matter what you do; if you complain, drag your feet, and have a crappy attitude, it's not going to be fun. Time for a reality check: mundane tasks do not end after high school. Do you think your parents enjoy going to work every day, changing diapers, filing taxes, or paying your phone bill? Probably not. Every privilege comes with responsibilities. We need to ditch the 'tude now, or we risk carrying this crummy attitude into the future.

> "The longer I live, the more I realize the impact of attitude on life. Attitude, to me, is more important than facts. It is more important than the past, than education, than money, than circumstances, than failures, than successes, than what other people think or say or do. It is more important than appearance, giftedness or skill. It will make or break a company... a church... a home. The remarkable thing is we have a choice every day regarding the attitude we will embrace for that day. We cannot change our past... we cannot change the fact that people will act in a certain way. We cannot change the inevitable. The only thing we can do is play on the one string we have, and that is our attitude ... I am convinced that life is 10 percent what happens to me and 90 percent how I react to it. And so it is with you ...we are in charge of our attitudes."
> —Charles Swindoll

Swindoll nails it. The majority of life is about how we react. I have this quote posted above my desk as a reminder of the daily decision I must make. Am I going to ponder the inadequacies of my present situation, or am I going to tackle challenges with the determination God provides? On your journey to graduation, you will have to take classes that don't interest you. But remember that your education is a privilege and a gift. So put on those positive pants, and hit the road running.

The key to avoiding the drag of high school is having a positive attitude. After waking up at 6 a.m., going through six classes, and trudging through practice, I understand that the last thing you want to do is study. But the reality is you *have* to do it if you want to pass the class, so you might as well have an optimistic outlook so you can get it over with!

Nixon had every reason to complain after not being able to spend time with his parents and walking several miles to school. However, instead of focusing on his challenges, he knew the blessing of his education trumped all shortcomings. It's all about attitude. We underestimate the power of changing our mindsets. As you'll hear in the hallway, it's common for students to complain. Be uncommon. Through your academics, take the narrow road by having a positive attitude toward your studies.

Don't get caught in the drag. Equip yourself with the proper mindset and acknowledge education for the blessing it is. We often search for a magical formula when the solution is simple. Learning how to overcome indifference is part of becoming a young adult. So suck it up, acknowledge that you're blessed, remember who it is all for, and just do it.

"Waiting until you FEEL like doing something may be the most common mistake you make."
—Rick Warren

Do all things without grumbling or disputing, that you may be blameless and innocent, children of God without blemish in the midst of a crooked and twisted generation, among whom you shine as lights in the world.
—Philippians 2:14:15

Knowledge is Power

Perhaps our schoolwork becomes such a burden because we fail to see it from a Biblical lens.

Have you ever read the book of Proverbs? It seems like God teaches me something every time I read this book. As we read what many call "the book of wisdom," we encounter the author's emphasis on the significance of knowledge, wisdom, insight, and understanding. Here are just a few examples:

> *[Wisdom] is more precious than jewels, and nothing you desire can compare with her.*
> —Proverbs 3:15

> *Take my instruction instead of silver, and knowledge rather than choice gold, for wisdom is better than jewels, and all that you may desire cannot compare with her.*
> —Proverbs 8:10-11

> *An intelligent heart acquires knowledge, and the ear of the wise seeks knowledge.*
> —Proverbs 18:15

Knowledge is power. Knowledge fosters our gifts to their fullest potential. The author of Proverbs puts incredible emphasis on chasing knowledge and wisdom, saying it is more valuable than precious stones. My translation: knowledge is more valuable than diamonds, Coach purses, and Aston Martins. The development of our brains is a key component of our future. God has given you things you're passionate about. High school is a time to discover those things, pursue them, and develop your skills to the best of your ability.

I'm not saying you have to love everything you study; I sure didn't. I'm thrilled that I will never have to take another math course. However, through my coursework, I have identified the strengths and weaknesses that I plan on developing for the future. For example, I was never a big science fan. Laboratory experiments and the periodic table never appealed to me. However, I discovered that reading, writing, speaking, and international relations fascinate me. I love being able to express myself through words. I could stare at world maps all day. Finding these passions has led me to study journalism with an emphasis on international relations. Instead of seeing your schoolwork as a burden, view knowledge as the power with which God uses you to change the world. Attitude and approach are game changers when it comes to our studies.

Prioritize and Organize

It goes without saying that your time is limited. You have to wake up at 6 a.m., stay in school well into the afternoon, keep up with clubs and sports, and, before you know it, you're at school until 6 p.m. Not to mention keeping up with schoolwork.

With a busy schedule, prioritizing and organizing are essential to success.

Prioritizing means acknowledging the most important objectives in light of your immediate situation and completing them. For example, on Monday, if you have an assignment due in a week and an exam on Thursday, study for the exam before working on your assignment.

Organization is also a lifesaver. It makes life much less hectic. With all the things you are expected to accomplish in high school, it's going to be nearly impossible to be successful if you're not organized. One of the easiest ways to stay organized is by using a calendar or a planner. If your school doesn't provide planners, invest in one. It's well worth the investment. Using the calendar in your phone is another option. And sticky notes also help!

You're assigned a ton of assignments throughout the course of a semester. Syllabi, along with papers and homework, can make for a pretty crowded notebook. Don't just stuff all your papers into the side of your textbook. Buy a binder, folders, page dividers, and organize your stuff. An organized binder will save you time and help you get started on your next assignment as soon as possible. We know that there are few things more demotivating than not being able to find your notes when you have to study for an exam.

Your time is limited. By prioritizing and organizing, you can make the most of your opportunities.

My Greatest Irony

Like newborn infants, long for the pure spiritual milk,
that by it you may grow up into salvation.
—1 Peter 2:2

I hated reading growing up.

Yes, those words are coming from the author himself. I was never one of those kids who spent their Saturday mornings with their faces stuffed in the latest edition of Junie B. Jones or Magic Tree House. I did everything I could to avoid reading. I remember pretending to read during silent reading time by hiding behind a pillow so I could look at pictures from Sports Illustrated. I was in for it once I got to high school, as I was expected to finish a book in a week. *To Kill a Mockingbird* in five days—really? I dreaded the idea of sitting still and following words on a page. And so most of my reading assignments turned into quality naps.

Distaste for books is often a result of subpar experiences in English class. You're forced to read books you are not interested in, and on top of everything, you have to write extensively on the material. These assignments contributed to the mindset I once had. However, let's not make a hasty judgment. It's too soon to call reading a nuisance just yet.

My junior year, the unthinkable happened; I developed an unexpected love for books. What changed? It all started with a book called *Crazy Love* by Francis Chan. I kept hearing about the book from people at my church. And once I learned that Chan and I shared the same haircut, I knew I had to give the book a shot.

It was one of the best decisions I ever made.

Crazy Love was the first book I read about something (or someone) I was actually interested in—Jesus. Chan quickly became one of my biggest role models and has taught me that books can be enjoyable.

Give reading another shot. My disdain disappeared when I began to read about my passions. I understand you're busy, and that you may have several books to finish by the end of the week. But the next time you are at Barnes & Noble, find an aisle with bookshelves that appeal to you. For some, it may be art history. For others, it could be the Invasion of Normandy. Maybe you have a desire to learn about different cultures, or the life of an athlete you admire. Whatever it is, I am cool with it—just no Cosmopolitan, please.

All jokes aside, here are some points that can help you rediscover a forgotten love.

Read Actively. If I'm not intentional, I'm the guy who can read a page and have no idea what I just read. Perhaps some of you can relate. For the longest time, I did not understand why I struggled with comprehension. Did I have a learning disability? Was I simply incompetent?

As I began to study for the LSAT, I was introduced to the idea of reading actively engaging and evaluating the material at hand. It is kind of like jumping to a pass in basketball. You don't stand flat-footed and wait for the ball to end up in your hands. Instead, you need to be quick on your feet and anticipate the pass.

In comparison, when we read, we should constantly evaluate the information and anticipate what's next. After every page, pause, and summarize what you just read. As enjoyable as books are, they're also time-consuming; active reading will help you make the most of your time!

Read with a Highlighter and Pen. Highlight key points, take notes, underline, star, do whatever helps you identify key points. Not only do marks help you actively read, but they also increase the book's value by making future reference easier. It's kind of like making a personal library of encyclopedias! When coming back to a novel, distinguishing highlighted points is much easier than flipping through an entire book.

Read a Variety of Genres. Not only will reading a variety of genres provide different perspectives, but they will also lessen bias in our judgments. I have had some of my greatest insights when reading books by atheist masterminds such as Christopher Hitchens and Sam Harris. Not because I agree with their viewpoints but because I was exposed to a whole new way of thinking. Variety forces us to think outside of the box and is a necessary push out of our literary comfort zones

Whatever your interest is, picking up a book is one of the most practical ways to increase brainpower. Have you ever noticed that most of the people who changed the world had a love for reading? Ben Franklin, Thomas Jefferson, and Nelson Mandela all professed that reading played a key role in their development. Let's take advantage of the benefits that come through the simple act of interpreting the written word.

Study Tips

"By failing to prepare, you are preparing to fail."
—Benjamin Franklin

If there were an academic discipline I wish I had developed more before I got to college, it would be study habits. I must admit I wasn't the best at preparing for exams. It wasn't that I was skipping class or failing. It was just that I was not putting in the necessary time and effort to perform to the best of my ability. This really bit me in the butt when I got to college, as I was expected to simultaneously study for three to four exams. Thankfully, I've learned from my mistakes, and I have learned a ton from those who especially excel in their studies. All of them have one thing in common: they are grounded and consistent in their preparation. As a college student, I have developed better habits. I've realized that effective study habits are the foundation upon which we build our academic success. Looking back, I wish someone would have sat me

down and shared a couple pointers on how to make the most of my time.

Avoid the Clutter. I would classify myself as a neat freak. I'm the guy who cleans his room often and color-coordinates his closet. However, when it comes to my desk, it's a whole new world. On any given day, you can find everything from letters to receipts to pictures on my desk. As if this wasn't messy enough, I have this terrible habit of dumping my backpack on my desk before I study. My desk ends up looking like the aftermath of a F5 super cell tornado. If you are already feeling overwhelmed by book reports and groups projects, a messy desk will only add to the anxiety. Clutter makes it easy to get distracted. Before starting a study session, clear your desk of all but the necessary tools. A clean workplace will reduce stress and help you stay focused.

Put the Phone Away. I know it is not an easy thing to do. But our phones are usually our worst enemy while studying. I still struggle with putting my phone away, but when I do, I study more efficiently. Don't just put your phone on vibrate. Turn it off. Put it under your bed. Give it to your mom or dad if that's what you have to do. Do whatever is necessary to help you focus. This goes for Facebook and Twitter, as well. Studying with social media in the background is like running a race with ankle weights—it holds us back from our full potential. And let's be real, sacrificing time away from your phone or social media isn't going to harm true friendships. For MacBook owners who find themselves distracted by the Internet, an app called Self Control can be a lifesaver. The program blocks selected websites for a designated period of time; so even if you shut down your laptop and restart it, you can't access the website!

Get Busywork out of the Way. I hate busywork. Hate it. I think

it's the biggest waste of time. However, more than likely you are going to have your fair share of it; so you might as well tighten up your attitude and get 'er done. When preparing to get your study grind on, get busywork—practice problems, questionnaires, short summaries—out of the way first. Even though it might be a nuisance, the feeling of finishing an assignment can provide a little extra motivation before you get going on your more difficult tasks.

Don't Lie Down. Just don't do it. I can't tell you how many times reviewing my notes lying on my bed turned into unexpected 3-4 hour naps. When you lay down, your body signals to your brain that it's time to shut down. Therefore, it is not the wisest decision to read your textbooks reclined on your couch; all the more so if you didn't get too much sleep the night before! Sit up straight, actively engage in the material, and focus on the task at hand.

The Value of Reviewing. "*I will do it later*" is one of the worst lies we tell ourselves. I have to give a shout-out to my mom for this one. She told me that when she was a chemistry teacher in South Korea, she always encouraged her students to review their notes at the end of the day. One, it is less likely you will return to or retain the material once the day is over. You want to take advantage of the information being fresh in your head. Two, taking the time to review will save you time in the long run. Studying bits and chunks consistently for a week is more beneficial than cramming a week's worth of material in one night. Cramming sucks. No one wants to lose sleep and be a walking zombie the day of an exam. Take the time to review. Consistency is key.

Be Honest with the Music. Whenever I study, Pandora "Yiruma" radio is my best friend. However, if I really need to concentrate, I must have silence. If I am trying to learn new material, any kind of noise is a distraction, whether it is the TV or the hum of a coffee shop. If you decide to listen to music on your study grind, be honest with yourself. Maybe the music helps during math problems but not when writing papers. Maybe a little Beethoven is good while reading, but not while finishing a lab report. Time is your most valuable resource; therefore, be wary of any distractions.

Coffee & Tea > Energy Drinks. Monster, Red Bull, Rockstar, and Noss become hot button items when midterms and finals roll around. However, the hazards of energy drinks involve more than jittery fingers. Studies show that energy drinks increase blood pressure, impair cognition, and disturb the heart's rhythm[vii]. FYI, your heart is not something you want to be messing with. The bad news does not end there. "*Sip all day, get decay,*" read the words of a poster at my dentist's office. Did you know that the pH level (acidity) of most energy drinks is closer to that of battery acid than Coke, sports drinks, or juice?[viii] Ew. I would rather drink something that is not going to deteriorate my gum lines. If you enjoy sipping on something when studying, ditch the 5 Hour Energy and grab a cup of coffee instead. Not only is mocha better for your overall health, but it's easier on your wallet! If you are not a fan of bitter taste, try a cup of Rooibos tea, a South African favorite. Chamomile tea is a good option as well. And don't forget to stay hydrated throughout the day!

The Finish Line

And now we approach a finish line, as well as a new beginning: the college process. The college process was the most faith-testing season of my high school experience. However, looking back, I can see how God used this time to draw me into deeper intimacy with Him.

A question pondered by philosophers seems to become all the more relevant as you apply it to college: *What is God's will for my life?*

Before tackling this question, let's not overlook truths about God's will that are clearly laid out in His word.

> *For this is the <u>will of my Father</u>, that everyone who*
> *looks on the Son and believes in him should have eternal*
> *life, and I will raise him up on the last day.*
> —John 6:40

*Do not be conformed to this world, but be transformed
by the renewal of your mind, that by testing you may
discern what is the <u>will of God</u>, what is good and
acceptable and perfect.*
—Romans 12:2

*For this is the <u>will of God</u>, your sanctification: that you
abstain from sexual immorality.*
—1 Thessalonians 4:3

*Rejoice always, pray without ceasing, give thanks in all
circumstances; for this is the <u>will of God</u> in Christ Jesus
for you.*
—1 Thessalonians 5:16-18

*For this is the <u>will of God</u>, that by doing good you
should put to silence the ignorance of foolish people.*
—1 Peter 2:15

These things we know because they are clear-cut. If you're not already obeying these things, then you're out of line with God's will. But then we get to the foggy areas, questions about God's will that are less clear-cut. *Where do I go to school? Whom do I marry? What kind of job should I pursue?* How do we respond when God's will is not so obvious?

In Genesis 1:27, we learn that we are made in the image of God. Later in 1 Corinthians 10:31, we learn that God is infinitely worthy of glory, in both mundane tasks such as eating and drinking and in the decisions we make about our future. Therefore, it's time to debunk a common misconception about the college process: college is about us.

College is *not* actually about us.

College—just like everything else in existence—is about Jesus. Your decision is just one small piece in God's grand puzzle of redemption.

It is tempting to treat the college process like a game of minesweeper; if I make one wrong decision, then my future is over. *What should I major in? What should I minor in? In state or out-of-state? How much financial aid should I apply for?* So many significant decisions are coming up fast and can cause tremendous anxiety.

Don't fall into the trap of thinking that your future is hopeless if you do not pick the right school. God is bigger than that, and logically, this would not make sense. Let's say you ended up attending the "wrong" school. Well, then that would cause someone else to be denied from their "right" school, resulting in a chain effect of askew college choices that would plague all of young adult America!

God's will is not a matter of right or wrong choices, but about delighting in Christ. In Psalm 37:4 we are told that when we delight in Jesus, His desires naturally take precedence over ours. We are to delight in Jesus in everything we do. Later in John 8:36, Christ reaffirms this idea when he says, *"So if the Son sets you free, you will be free indeed."*

Not only is Christ bigger than our decision-making, but He has also promised, *"that for those who love God all things work together for good"* (Romans 8:28). In Christ, we have true freedom. In Christ, we take comfort in communing with the one who holds the universe intact. This does not mean we blatantly do things contradictory to Scripture. Anyone who truly understands grace does not make a practice of sinning (Romans 6:1-2). Freedom in Christ is acknowledging that even though we cannot yet perceive the next chapter, we trust the One who wrote the story.

Are you uncertain if you will get into the nursing program? That is okay. Do you not know if college is even a financial option? That is okay. Continue to pursue Jesus with all your heart. His desires for you will be revealed as you continue to walk by faith. Trust Him and delight in the freedom that is only possible through Jesus Christ.

Here are some practical tips to keep in mind prior-to and during the college process:

Research Prospective Schools. I had a skewed perception of Michigan State University before I became a Spartan. However, my viewpoint changed once I learned more about their College of Communication Arts and Sciences. I realized that even though I might not have liked their football team growing up, MSU offered the programs that were best fitted for my endeavors. Don't judge a school by its mascot. Take the time to learn about your prospective schools. What's the curriculum like for your major? Do your advanced placement class credits transfer in? Big campus or little campus? Greek life? Do you qualify for financial aid? What's their campus safety rating?

You're about to drop several thousands dollars on your education. The least you can do is ensure it's a good investment. One more thing, school pride is always a plus, but it shouldn't be a significant influence in your decision. There is more to a school than its football program. Too often, factors such as athletics or Greek life have more influence than the education you're paying for.

Get on that Standardized Test Grind. As if you needed something else to add to your schedule. Why take the time to study for something every junior dreads? Because your ACT or SAT score has significant influence on your future college, and your future college has significant influence on what you will do for the rest of your life. Don't be afraid to take the test more than once. Most students tend to get better results the second or third time around. It's just like anything else in life; you have to work for it. Even though I love MSU, there is always a part of me that wishes I had worked a little bit harder. One or two points higher on my score could have opened up a whole new world of prospective schools and scholarships. Whether it is buying a study book or enrolling in a class, how you prepare is up to you. Suffer a little now so you will have no regrets later!

Résumé Building. The time to start building your college résumé is not halfway through your junior year; it is when you walk through the doors as a freshman. Colleges like to see consistency in the activities you are involved in. They want to see self-motivated, dedicated, hard-working individuals who will bring those same qualities to their campuses.

Get involved. Find an activity or club that interests you. Build relationships with teachers. Even though it is hard to believe, they have lives, as well. Not only can they teach you lessons outside of the classroom, but they are excellent options for letters of recommendation. As cool as it is to be accepted to your dream school, remember that it's not about the name or future salary. Do what you love. Be well rounded, but more importantly, be who God has created you to be.

Back it up. You are talking to someone who enrolled at the school he thought he would never go to. Apply to your schools of choice but make sure you have a backup school that you are confident you can get into. You don't want to be stuck in the middle of April wishing you had more options. Rejection happens, and you need to be prepared. The application process is competitive, but God is in control. I ended up at my backup school, and now I cannot imagine being anywhere else! Still not sure? There is nothing wrong with going to community college for a few years. You can save money and complete basic requirements before heading off to a four-year institution.

Shine. When you apply to a school, remember there are thousands of others in the application pool with you. You don't want to be another bystander in the crowd. What sets you apart from other students? What qualities or experiences do you have to offer to this university? Why should they accept you over another candidate who has the same GPA and standardized test scores? Shine in your application essays. This is the time for you to express yourself and show the admissions office who you are and what you stand for.

Chapter Six
Year Two: Sophomore Year

Everyone then who hears these words of mine and does them will be like a wise man who built his house on the rock. And the rain fell, and the floods came, and the winds blew and beat on that house, but it did not fall, because it had been founded on the rock. And everyone who hears these words of mine and does not do them will be like a foolish man who built his house on the sand. And the rain fell, and the floods came, and the winds blew and beat against that house, and it fell, and great was the fall of it.
—Matthew 7:24-27

Did you know that the Latin root of "sophomore" can be translated to "wise fool?" Sound like an oxymoron? It's funny because this period of high school is much like an oxymoron in and of itself. The exciting, new beginnings of being a freshman are in the past; however, you are not quite an upperclassman yet. You are stuck between two realities and are about to face a whirlwind of change in the future. Are you prepared to respond?

Treat this year as the cornerstone that will support the remainder of your high school experience. It is the time to develop good habits because life is only going to pick up from here. Time flies. Did you know that's a Biblical concept? James 4:14 describes our lives as a mist, here one second, and gone the next, evaporating quicker than the time it takes to take another breath.

Do not waste the unique opportunities in front of you because you are too focused on what is down the road. The driver's license will come, prom will be a blast in its due time, and believe it or not, you will be graduating before you know it. For now, you have the once-in-a-lifetime opportunity to be a sophomore in high school. There is no need to be in a hurry to grow up. Too often, we seek an unrealistic expectation of the future. We trick ourselves into thinking that if we get to a certain point or past a certain obstacle, everything will slow down and get easier. The problem is, if you have made it this far, you might have realized that life doesn't get any easier as you get older. I mean, how many times have you told yourself, "I'll do it later"? We must resist the urge to fall into this trap that never leads to contentment. Instead, we must learn to be content in the present and take advantage of what is right in front of us.

Former UCLA men's basketball coach John Wooden said it eloquently: "Failing to prepare is preparing to fail." A 400m dash is not won or lost in the home stretch. What happens at the finish line is a result of what an athlete did in the offseason. It's the 7 a.m. lifts, ice baths, and the hours poured into perfecting your technique that determines who makes it past regionals and onto the state finals. Victory is in the preparation. We want to be like the wise man Jesus talked about, who prepared for the storms before the dark clouds rolled in (Matthew 7:24-27).

You are about to go to war.

This is the time when high school starts to pick up. As your reign as an upperclassmen approaches, grades get more serious, friend groups separate, and the narrow road becomes narrower. Not to mention that college decisions linger on the horizon. What is your foundation? Where are you finding your identity? What brings you joy every day? Is there anything holding you back from being wholeheartedly surrendered to

God? Junior year is right around the corner, and for most, the third year of high school is the most difficult. When the storms come, are you going to be the wise man, or the foolish man that Jesus talked about? It all depends on your actions today.

Now is the time to develop the discipline of intentionality. Start practicing good study habits. You'll thank me later, I promise. Your workload may not seem heavy at the moment, but advanced placement classes and standardized testing will pack a punch in the near future. It'll be much easier to adjust to the rigors if you have already begun to learn how to be disciplined. But most importantly, the discipline of intentionality is best applied in spending time with God in His Word. There's no better investment; the benefits are eternal!

Now is the time to try new things. If freshman year did not go too hot, consider this an opportunity to redefine yourself. Go out for the golf team. Join the French club. Audition for the spring musical. Meet new friends, and add experience to your résumé.

Now is the time to start hanging out with the right group of friends. We're always influenced by those we spend the most time with, whether we realize it or not. The party life is going to start to creep in. There's a good chance some of your friends might go off the deep end. It can be tempting to get sucked right into the current. Therefore, find people who appreciate you for who you are and encourage you to follow Christ. More importantly, *be* the kind of person you would want to be friends with. We can't neglect Jesus' second greatest commandment: to "*love your neighbor as yourself*" (Matthew 22:39).

It's also not a bad time to jump-start that reading habit. Not only is reading comprehension a component of standardized test scores, but reading also complements your overall academic success. And it is not a skill you can develop overnight. Start off with a book that sparks your interest, and go from there. Books are everyday tools that reap extraordinary benefits!

Wishing you had done more is one of the worst feelings. Sure, it takes more time and effort to build a house on rock rather than sand. But when the storm starts to rage, you'll be grateful that you went the extra mile.

Chapter Seven
The Narrow Road Through The Party Scene

No temptation has overtaken you that is not common to man. God is faithful, and he will not let you be tempted beyond your ability, but with the temptation he will also provide the way of escape, that you may be able to endure it.
—1 Corinthians 10:13

Heads Up

High School is a time when you start learning more about what the world has to offer.

In this chapter, I want to address the temptation of drinking alcohol. The whole boozing fad caught me off-guard as I transitioned into my upperclassman years. I had seen the movies where kids got hammered at parties. Of course, there was that group in my grade known for going wild over the weekends. But as a freshman and sophomore, getting tipsy wasn't quite the thing to do—yet. Things quickly changed as I got older. The narrow road appeared narrower and the wide road that much wider. More of my friends started to drink, and more of my friends began to do the things they said they would never do a few years ago. Temptations arise in many forms; I'm sure you have encountered a few of them. You must make the decision to not only resist this temptation, but fight against it with the Sword of the Spirit (Ephesians 6:17). Besides sexual temptation, perhaps no other lure of Satan has led to students' downfalls across the country and across the globe.

Hell Hates You

I still remember the heartbreak of watching my friends suppress their God-given potential. This is what Satan wants. You must come to a realization that there is an enemy who is trying to take you down.

Hell hates you. Hell is aware of your potential influence and is trying stop you anyway it can.

> *For we do not wrestle against flesh and blood, but against the rulers, against the authorities, against the cosmic powers over this present darkness, against the spiritual forces of evil in the heavenly places.*
> —Ephesians 6:12

> *Beloved, I urge you as sojourners and exiles to abstain from the passions of the flesh, which wage war against your soul.*
> —1 Peter 2:11

Taking the narrow road means you have a target on your back. By now, you should realize that following Christ is not a half-hearted endeavor. Your generation is caught in the middle of a war between God and Satan. The fight is on, and human souls are at stake. We know who wins in the end. But until then, we must stand firm in the faith because the enemy is trying to trip us up.

Hell hates us, but we often find ourselves believing its lies. "Not good enough." "Not pretty enough." However, Jesus *is* enough. This is not going to be a chapter of underage drinking statistics. Numbers are significant, however, this generation does not need more rules to live by, but a calling to live for. Living for a cause more significant than us—that is the essence of the gate that leads to life. The only statistic that matters is this: your influence + your student body population = the amount of people who need to see someone (You!) stand unashamed for the truth. And let's be real, numbers won't keep someone from picking up a Heineken on Friday night.

Jesus, The Relatable Savior

In the face of temptation, I developed a deeper appreciation for the fact that Jesus is such the relatable Savior. Hebrews describes him as *"one who in every respect has been tempted as we are, yet without sin"* (Hebrews 4:15). Take great comfort in this. Jesus can relate to us, no matter what the evil one throws at us.

In Matthew 4:1-11, Jesus is exhausted after spending 40 days and 40 nights wandering in the desert. Satan not only tries to tempt Jesus, but comes when Jesus was physically weak. I know I have been there. How much easier is it to snap at your little brother after a long day? Jesus endured temptations, but never sinned. Sounds like a Savior I want to know.

Then Jesus was led up by the Spirit into the wilderness to be tempted by the devil. And after fasting forty days and forty nights, he was hungry. And the tempter came and said to him, "If you are the Son of God, command these stones to become loaves of bread." But he answered, "It is written, "Man shall not live by bread alone, but by every word that comes from the mouth of God." Then the devil took him to the holy city and set him on the pinnacle of the temple and said to him, "If you are the Son of God, throw yourself down, for it is written," 'He will command his angels concerning you,' and "On their hands they will bear you up, lest you strike your foot against a stone." Jesus said to him, "Again it is written, 'You shall not put the Lord your God to the test.' " Again, the devil took him to a very high mountain and showed him all the kingdoms of the world and their glory. And he said to him, "All these I will give you, if you will fall down and worship me." Then Jesus said

to him, "Be gone, Satan! For it is written," 'You shall worship the Lord your God and him only shall you serve.' " Then the devil left him, and
behold, angels came and were ministering to him.

You can pull so many points from this story. Density is one of Scripture's innumerable beauties. A single passage of scripture could lead to hours upon hours of interpretation. Break down this passage on your own time, and see what the Spirit teaches you. For now, let us concentrate on three points that specifically relate to the issue of temptation.

The Devil is sneaky—incredibly sneaky. Satan attempts to use the Word of God as part of his scheme to tempt Jesus; how ironically evil! Then again, this kind of mischief is nothing new for the mustached man in a red suit, equipped with a pitchfork. Cartoons portray the darndest things. Unfortunately, the devil is more than what we see in our Saturday morning cartoons. He is sly. Don't expect him to show up in your school cafeteria. He is more intelligent than people realize. Most likely he will find an alternate route, where we will not expect him, as he did in the Garden of Eden. Satan did not show up in the Garden in a red suit with a pitchfork. No, he was slippery, literally! He showed up in a way Adam and Eve never expected, disguised as one of God's creation.

He tries to sell the lie that drinking is a regular part of high school. *"Everyone else is doing it,"* he says. If he can get you to think that it is *"just a drink"* or *"no one will find out"* he has already won. Keep your guard up. Stand firm. What may sound like a harmless decision could be the whisper of a *"roaring lion, seeking someone to devour"* (1 Peter 5:8).

Jesus' focus was heavenward. The devil tried to tempt Jesus with what seemed good to the immediate senses. Satan never thinks long-term, but Jesus does. Satan does not want to think long-term because he knows that he doesn't win in the big picture. Jesus knows He is going to win in the end. Even in the desert, He realized Satan's offer wasn't all it was cracked up to be.

When the temptation to drink emerges, it sounds at first like it

71

will be a great time. *"Everyone else is doing it." "One time can't hurt." "It will be fun."* Sure, it may seem fun for the night, but what about tomorrow morning? Next week? Does it really satisfy? Those who drink away the weekends end up like a dog chasing its tail. We must remember the road that leads to life is narrow. We must not think like everyone else thinks. The narrow road does not appeal to the immediate senses, because the immediate never satisfies. We take the narrow road because temporary emotional sacrifice is eternally worth the cost.

Jesus waged war on temptation by memorizing Scripture. Jesus unashamedly responded to temptation by submitting to the Word of God. In the face of adversity, He refused to rely on human wisdom or strength. His focus was heavenward, toward His Father. He realized that God's promises were greater than anything the devil could offer.

Notice that Jesus quoted the Bible in its original context. Hence, we see the value of memorizing the Word of God. If the Son of God confronted temptation with the recitation of God's Word, then who are we to neglect the discipline of Scripture memorization? Satan tried to nitpick passages to get his way. See how sneaky he is? Be on guard. The Bible calls him the *"father of lies"* (John 8:44). Here, we see why.

Satan quoted Scripture for his own selfish gain. It is easy to be critical of the enemy, but we can easily make the same mistake if we're not careful. How do you respond when temptation arises? Do you simply look in the Bible for "feel good" passages? Or do you yearn for the truth that will help you stand firm, even if it might sting a little? How do you tend to view Scripture in those occasions? Instead of reading Scripture to glorify Him, we can mistakenly use verses for emotional gain. We can end up reading the Bible to simply feel good about ourselves instead of delighting in Jesus for all of He is worth. Responding to temptation in a Biblical manner means embracing the fact that you have everything you need in Christ, through the power of His Word. Not just the encouragement of the Psalms, but also the conviction in Romans. Not just Philippians 4:13 and Jeremiah 29:11, but also the surrounding verses talking about God's provision to the church at Philippi and the Babylonian exile. Wielding the Word of God—the Sword of the Spirit—

is the ultimate responsibility. And if we are not careful, we can end up creating a false depiction of Jesus.

Jesus modeled the appropriate response in the face of temptation: absolute submission to the Word of God in its proper framework; having faith that God's commandments are to guard us from harm.

The Reasons

Acceptance, pleasure, peer pressure, there are a plethora of reasons that contribute to the phenomenon of high school drinking. During my tenure, I encountered three common reasons why people decided to go along with the crowd. Interestingly, all the reasons had one thing alike: seeking something from the world that we can only find in Jesus.

"Drinking is a part of growing up. I just want to see what it is all about."

It is only natural to be curious, right? You want to know what all the hype is about and whether drinking is all that it is cracked up to be. I have been there. I have wondered about a lot of things. I have speculated what it would feel like to get drunk. I have pondered how different my life would be if I did not grow up in Europe for six years. I am also in an endless debate with myself whether or not I will have wings in Heaven. I am an extremely curious person, as I am sure you are as well. This kind of thinking is endless. However, we must realize there are more things we will fail to experience than things we will. You have to decide what is worth your time. In fact, the Word of God warns us against our own curiosity.

> *The heart is deceitful above all things, and desperately sick;*
> *who can understand it?*
> —Jeremiah 17:9

We need to be careful with our own curiosity. Being aware of our sin nature requires us to evaluate the motivation behind our curiosity. If you really are that eager to find out what it feels like to get drunk, you do not have to go far for an answer. Look at the world around us, a world where alcohol never satisfies the continual thirst of a man's soul. Earlier we talked about Jesus' long-term focus in the face of temptation compared to the devil's immediate but unfulfilling bargains. In the Facebook pictures, tweets, and stories on Monday morning, it might seem like your classmates had a great time. But until they drink from the cup that Jesus offers, they are caught in an endless spiral. They are seeking from the world a fulfillment they can only get from God. You are not missing out on much. Drink instead from the cup Jesus offers you. Faith in Him leads to true, continuous satisfaction.

> *If anyone thirsts, let him come to me and drink. Whoever believes in me, as the Scripture has said, 'Out of his heart will flow rivers of living water.*
> —John 7:37-38

"It's the best way to have fun!" The problem with alcohol is that it is a beverage and a drug. The question is, what are you using it for? First off, it is illegal for high school students to consume alcohol, and God commands us to submit to legal authority (Romans 13:1-2). Second, the reason most students drink isn't to responsibly use alcohol, but to abuse it. You wouldn't chug water until you puked. You wouldn't drink orange juice to the point you had trouble functioning the next morning. At least, I hope not.

To many, drinking provides the best means of having a good time. It is about getting crazy and going along with the status quo. The messages you get from movies and Lil' Wayne sure do reinforce the cause. The bottom line is, though, that it is not worth it. There will be a time in your life when alcohol can be consumed responsibly. However, in these years it is not worth the risk. Is a bitter drink—which in my opinion doesn't taste half as good as cherry coke—really worth risking a criminal offense? Do you really want to risk starting off your young adult life with a criminal record? I had friends who lost college scholarships because of MIPs. Forfeiting free college tuition for a drink does not seem worth it to me. More than that, does it even satisfy what you were looking for in the first place? Sure, it may be fun for a bit, but all these beverages offer is temporary fulfillment.

People always think the grass is greener on the other side. For example, Novi, the town I went to high school in, is super suburbia. Subdivisions, shopping malls, and a lot of wealthy families. However, many of my classmates would complain, "There is nothing to do in Novi." Perhaps this is something you hear at your school. I guess it really depends on what people mean by "things to do." It is inevitable that you will get used to your hometown after a few years. However, for the most part, students just aren't looking hard enough. There are numerous ways to have fun without drinking. During high school, I found plenty of ways to have fun without getting in trouble.

These were some of my favorite ways to spend my weekends: Get together with a group of friends and just chill. Plan a game night. Go see a movie. Go on an adventure. Explore a neighboring town you have never been to. Go to the mall. Play Ultimate Frisbee. Learn to play an instrument. TP your youth pastors house. There are scores of options available to you. Make your own fun. Be a kid. Don't underestimate the results of your own creativity.

"I need to escape reality." You don't have to go farther than the evening news to realize this world is messed up. Some of you are going through difficult times. High school can challenge all aspects of life. The brokenness we experience leads us to seek a solution, something to ease the pain. And then comes the devil, telling us a drink or inebriated state of consciousness can help suppress the heartache. However, even in movies that portray this scene, does alcohol end up providing the sought-after gratification?

I hope you are noticing a common theme. People want something. Humans desire some sort of satisfaction. We all search for fulfillment until we find Jesus; it is how we were designed. Timothy Keller puts it eloquently.

"Indeed (as it was just objected) just because we *feel* the desire for a steak dinner doesn't mean we will get it. However, while hunger doesn't prove that the particular meal desired will be procured, doesn't the appetite for food in us mean that food exists? Isn't it true that innate desires correspond to real objects that can satisfy them, such as sexual desire (corresponding to sex), physical appetite (corresponding to food), tiredness (corresponding to sleep), and relational desires (corresponding to friendship)? Doesn't the unfulfillable longing evoked by beauty qualify as an innate desire? We have a longing for joy, love, and beauty that no amount or quality of food, sex, friendship, or success can satisfy. We want something that nothing in this world can fulfill. Isn't that at least a clue that this "something" that we want exists? This unfulfillable longing, then, qualifies, as a deep, innate human desire, and that makes it a major clue that God is there."[ix]

Our hearts are missing something. Our souls are missing something. Every fiber of our being cries out for a love this world cannot give. Blaise Pascal and C.S. Lewis put it this way,

> "There is a God shaped vacuum in the heart of every man which cannot be filled by any created thing, but only by God, the Creator, made known through Jesus."
> —Blaise Pascal

> "If I find in myself a desire which no experience in this world can satisfy, the most probable explanation is that I was made for another world."
> —C.S. Lewis

Scriptural interpretation of alcohol consumption can be debated. Some say all alcohol consumption is a sin. Others claim there is nothing wrong as long as it is consumed responsibly. Nevertheless, it is clear drunkenness is a sin. Ephesians 5:18 commands us not to "not to get drunk with wine [that] is debauchery" but instead be "filled with the Spirit." Drunkenness is a state where we are filled and controlled by something other than the Spirit of God. It impairs our decision-making and replaces the role God is meant to hold in our lives.

Why does God offer the Spirit as a means of fulfillment in

contrast to drunkenness? I have found that being filled with the Holy Spirit is exhilaration unlike anything of the natural world. No, I am not talking about an emotional occurrence, a high, or charismatic dogma. I am talking about the immeasurable joy of being satisfied in Jesus. He is what our souls have thirsted for all along. For the student who feels hopeless about their future, let the Spirit satisfy you. For the brother who is tired of seeking approval from parents, coaches, teachers, and girls, let the Spirit satisfy you. For the sister who struggles with her self-image, let the Spirit satisfy you. You will face hardship in these four years. There will be the whisper that suggests other means of gratification. But I pray that when temptation comes, your focus would be upon Jesus, the author and finisher of your faith (Hebrews 12:2). May you find fulfillment in His love. Jesus, only Jesus.

Colossians 1:16 says that "all things were created *through* him and *for* him." You were made to be satisfied by God. If you are going through a rough time and seek a way to deal with your problems, ask yourself "What is truly going to satisfy?" Not just the answer to our current difficulties, but the answer to the longing we have had since we were born. The love of Jesus Christ is the only thing that always has and continues to satisfy. Isn't the emptiness in you, the longing that no amount of success, beauty, or friendship can satisfy, only proof that such a Savior exists?

He does.

This world will never satisfy. People are looking for something. Perhaps you are too. And the only drink that brings true contentment is the cup Jesus offers.

> *Jesus said to her, "Everyone who drinks of this water will be thirsty again, but whoever drinks of the water that I will give him will never be thirsty again. The water that I will give him will become in him a spring of water welling up to eternal life."*
> —John 4:13-14

You Are Who You Hang Out With

"Show me a man's friends, and I will show you his future."
—Anonymous

"You are a mixture of the five people you spend the most time with."
—Anonymous

The people we spend the most time with have a significant influence on us. Those we talk on the phone with before going to bed, the groups we hang out with on Friday and Saturday nights, the people we do life with…these are people whose attitudes we will conform to.

Drinking is already a common temptation; why make it harder by surrounding yourself with negative influences? Compare being at a party to going to church on Sunday. Don't the ways of the world appeal more when those around you indulge in its pleasures? Isn't it easier to raise your hands during worship when everyone else is doing the same? It's easier to compromise when those around you don't share the same values. But on the flip side, you are encouraged to stand firm in your faith when you are surrounded by other unashamed believers. Our friends are an indication of our future. The people who we allow to influence us are part of our personal responsibility.

My favorite illustration in Scripture is Psalm 23, where our relationship to God is compared to that of a shepherd and his sheep.[x] Now, if you have been around sheep before, you might think they are stupid. They sit around, eat grass all day, and get eaten by wolves. Growing up in England, I saw hoards of dead sheep everywhere around the countryside; on the side of the road, by the rocks on the river, and at the bottom of ledges. I assumed their stupidity led them to their deaths. While sheep may not be the brightest of species, their feebleness is not rooted in a lack of mental capacity. Instead, they are designed to reflect man's relationship with God.

Sheep are not stupid, but dependent.[xi]

Sheep are one of the only animals that are desperately dependent on their leader[2]. Essentially, sheep will die without the guidance of a shepherd who is also influencing the rest of the herd. Sheep can't even drink water by themselves! Because if their wool is too long, it gets wet, too heavy, and the sheep will drown. Now, if we are compared to sheep, we must realize we are not as strong as we think. In fact, we are significantly weaker than we would like to believe. We are easily influenced by our peers and can be led astray if we are not cautious. We are going to be influenced by our peers regardless of who they are or what they believe. Therefore, we must surround ourselves with those who will stand firm with us on the narrow road.

In the area of temptation, hungry wolves are trying to take you down. If you desire the narrow road, yet have a close association with those who get trashed on the weekends, it is not going to work. We are too weak and dependent. If we can observe socially and scripturally that we are easily influenced, we must be cautious of the type of people we hang out with.

On the narrow road you are going in a direction completely counterculture. It is significantly easier to get discouraged. That is why I cannot stress enough the importance of engaging in Biblical community, with those who will inspire you "to love and good works" (Hebrews 10:24). Do not go through this journey alone. Spending time with the wrong crowd will hinder your endeavors to live a life pleasing to God.

I am not saying we should force ourselves into a Christian bubble. I am not saying all we should do is hangout with our Christian buddies, watch VeggieTales, and take communion together five times a week. Sheltering yourself from the world can be as harmful as associating yourself with the world. If you love the world, you damage the reputation and ministry of the church. If you shelter yourself from the world, you become numb to the needs of discipleship and witnessing.

Jesus commanded us to make disciples and be His witnesses, both of which require us to strategically and intentionally place ourselves within society (Matthew 28:18-20, Acts 1:8). We are not to be in the world for our own pursuits, but for the advancement of the Gospel. Being a runner, I love the analogies of competition presented throughout the

New Testament, particularly Hebrews 12:1-3. In the second part of verse two, Paul identifies two potential obstacles that hold us back in our walks with Christ. The first is sin, obviously. Then he says to "*lay aside every weight.*" Unrepentant sin restrains us in our race of eternal significance; however, there may also be things that are not necessarily sin, but still suppress us from our full potential.

For some of us it may be busyness. It is not a bad thing to work hard. However, when our work consumes our lives, it can become a plague to our relationship with God. For others it may be a resource that has been given us. Take a phone as an example. My iPhone has been an incredible resource, not only for school but also for keeping in touch with friends. However, there have been times where my phone has become a distraction, while I study, write, or am in a group situation where I should be interacting with others.

Your "weight" likely could be your influences, the people who are closest to you. Who do you spend the most time with? Who are the people who know the most about you? Who are the brothers or sisters you can call when tragedy strikes? These are the ones who are going to influence you, and you need to choose them wisely. Because even though hanging out with them in and of itself might not be a sin, they effect they have on your attitude, words, and decisions could hold you back from running with God.

Strike a balance between being in the world but not of the world. Ask yourself which way the transforming influence is flowing. Are your unbelieving friends being convicted and loved by the way you talk and live your life? Or are you being tempted to suppress the value of holiness and obedience to God's Word? A practical way of finding this balance is getting involved in your school. We will talk about this more in the sports and extracurricular activities chapter. For the time being, figure out ways you could express your passions outside the classroom. This way you have the opportunity to honor God through your passion, but also the chance to meet non-Christians.

Another Fuzzy Issue

I was open to the suggestions of my peers as I wrote this book because high school is a different experience for everybody. There was a question that came up repetitively and still comes up now as I am in college.

"Is it all right to go to parties, but not drink?"

I used to think there was nothing wrong with going to parties to hang out but not drink. But as I matured in my understanding of Scripture, my stance changed.

I don't think it is wise to go to a party just to "hang out."

I used to justify myself by saying I was being a light where it was dark, so I decided to go to parties to spend time with my friends, but not drink. After all, I did not want to be a loner on Friday and Saturday night, nor did I want my friends to think I was looking down on them. I soon learned that my thinking was detrimental.

It all goes back to influence. You have to realize that there is power in your presence. Ask yourself, how does a room change when you walk into it? How does your company affect others? Is it positive? Your presence is a statement to others of what you stand for.

Just as positive influence builds up, adverse company tears down. Paul sums it up in his first letter to the Corinthian church.

Do not be deceived: "Bad company ruins good morals."
—1 Corinthians 15:33

Yes, we are called to be a light, but this does not include being responsible for the folly of others. Otherwise, it would be impossible to carry out our own ministry because we would be too busy dealing with the mistakes of others.

During my freshman and sophomore years, I struggled with the conflict of desiring to be a light and desiring the approval of others. *"God, use me as a light, but please don't take away all my friends!" "God, help me to be a positive influence, but please make sure people like me!"* I wanted the best of both worlds. I wanted to be a light but I was also concerned with the opinions of others. So this is what I would do: I would go to parties, but I wouldn't drink. Instead, I sat in the back and made small talk with those who were sober. When things got wild, I would play Angry Birds for the rest of the night and leave smelling like cranberry vodka. It wasn't fun.

Not only was it not fun, but I soon realized my actions were not helping the people I thought I was ministering to.

On Sunday morning, I logged onto Facebook and found myself tagged in pictures from the night before. At first I was cool with it because of all the trouble I had gone through gelling my hair and wearing nice clothes. However, what I found next convicted me. In some of the pictures I was tagged in, my friends had put captions of Bible verses and quotes referring to my faith. Nothing derogatory, just your everyday Jesus freak comments. It hit me. Not only did my friends know I was a Christian, but they were beginning to associate the things I stood for with the things they were stood for.

My friends were coming to the conclusion that I approved of their actions. Not because I took a drink, but simply by my presence. I realized in my attempts to witness, I was pursuing man's approval above God's. I wanted to be close with some of my friends who weren't saved, yet I still wanted to follow Christ. I realized that simply by standing there, I was approving of their actions. That wasn't going to work.

Following Christ on the narrow road may very well mean giving up some relationships. I had to make a tough decision. Was I going to trust God for other opportunities to witness to my friends, or was I going to live a double life and follow Him half-heartedly? Realistically, did I really think Jesus would go into these environments and just stand there? Following the Spirit's leading is one thing, but I completely forgot about good old "What would Jesus do?"

We are to be lights in the world; however, Scripture makes it clear we are not supposed to look like the world. The Bible gives a stern warning in James 4:4 that those who are friends with the world are enemies of God. Scripture goes on to call us citizens of Heaven, "*sojourners,*" and "*exiles*" (Philippians 3:20, 1 Peter 2:11). We are not supposed to fit in.

But wait, didn't Jesus sit down and eat with tax collectors and sinners? Aren't we supposed to be like Christ? While Jesus spent sufficient time with unbelievers, he was not just hanging out. His actions

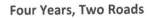
were strategic and intentional. He was not spending time with people for retweets and Facebook likes. Jesus' presence prompted action.

Take His encounter with Zacchaeus in Luke 19. Zacchaeus was a chief tax collector. Tax collectors were Jews who worked for the Roman government. They were viewed as traitors because they would often take more money than was required and pocket it for themselves. Zacchaeus was sinful, no doubt, and he certainly did not have the best reputation.

However, we see how Jesus' presence provoked Zacchaeus to repentance. Although He had become famous for His miracles and teaching, Christ's presence impelled Zacchaeus to climb the sycamore tree and realize his need for a Savior.

This does not mean Jesus accepts sinful behavior. He was not slow to call out depravity during His earthly ministry. In fact, He called out sin extensively, explaining all the while how the world hates Him because He testifies its works are evil (John 7:7). Jesus was deliberate in His demeanor; much like how the author of Ecclesiastes says there is a time and a place for everything (Ecclesiastes 3:1-8).

In Luke 19, we see Jesus' mercy and grace to the likes of sinners as well as the intentionality of His ministry. Instead of tolerating Zacchaeus' ways, Christ strategically presented himself, because He knew there was power in His presence. Likewise, for those on the narrow road, His spirit gives us the same authority. The Spirit also gives us discernment to the situations where our presence would be the most effective. Yes, we are to be burning lights wherever God calls us, but first we must walk with the wisdom that only He can provide.

Your most effective ministry isn't going to be at parties. It is going to be at practice, Friday night football games, the lunch table, student council, whatever you are involved with. Your ministry will come into fruition as you do life with the people God has placed in your life.

In all we do, let us imitate Christ. Jesus discipled through living everyday life with His 12 disciples. He taught them, but He also ate with them. He walked on water, but He also prayed for them. Be genuine like He was. You don't have to go far to realize people love genuineness and despise fakeness. This isn't something new. Ever noticed Jesus' reaction to the Pharisees?

A genuine demeanor toward your classmates, despite their behavior, can be a powerful witness, as we see in Jesus' account with Zacchaeus.

Besides, your ministry wouldn't be effective in a party-like atmosphere. Because let's be honest, the people you would try to talk to wouldn't remember a thing you said the next morning.

The Power of Accountability

So, now that we know we are easily influenced, we need to choose to be around people who will sharpen us into the man or woman we are destined to be (Proverbs 27:17). We need brothers and sisters who are on the same mission as we are and will do what is necessary to keep us on track.

Perhaps you have heard about accountability before. An accountability partner is someone who holds you accountable to God's standards for your life. It is the idea of having fellow brothers and sisters who will love us even if it means being tough at times.

Accountability relationships can be life-changing; I know it has been for me. Connor was my accountability partner in high school. After meeting on a mission trip to Jamaica, we decided to keep each other accountable in our sexual purity. We would meet every other week and discuss our walks with God. Sometimes we met at each other's houses, other times we would grab Coney Island. We would ask each other some tough questions.

"Were you staring at any girls lustfully in the gym this week?"
"Did you watch anything on the computer or the television that challenged your integrity?" *"Did you cross boundaries when you hung out with your girlfriend?"*

This sort of conversation sounds awkward, and it is initially. When you are discussing the innermost parts of the heart, it is going to be uncomfortable. But it is absolutely necessary. The benefits of openhearted honesty are infinitely worth a few occasions of discomfort. The result is an intimate brotherhood or sisterhood, sharpened as a result of God's Word.

It is impossible to live on the narrow road if personal comfort is a high priority. There were times when Connor and I had to say some tough things to each other. Harsh words were occasionally necessary. However, there were also times we celebrated victory together! Candy and slurpee splurges were often the result of a maintained period of integrity. I am blessed to say our accountability partnership is still going strong today! Accountability has encouraged and sharpened me. It will provide much needed encouragement through the treacherous stretches of high school. Here are a couple guidelines to help you get started.

100% Honesty. Accountability only works if you are willing to be brutally honest. Seems like it should go without saying, however, it goes back to the discomfort issue. Some of you might be hesitant to share personal matters, and that is okay. Get to know each other first. You don't have to discuss your greatest struggles right off the bat. However, accountability relationships are probably second to boyfriend/girlfriend relationships in terms of intimacy. APs are different than other relationships because of its focus. They are not out solely to have fun with each other or make each other happy. What's the point of patting someone on the back if they are drowning in sin? APs love one another in the truth of Scripture by saying what we need to hear rather than what we want to hear.

Plan Ahead and Be Intentional. Figure out a time and place every week or every other week where you will meet with your accountability partner. You're not the only one with a busy schedule. Life is hectic for just about everyone. Therefore, be all the more intentional about meeting with one another (Hebrews 10:25). Pick a time and place and make each other a priority. Remember, these times can be life changing!

I once again acknowledge temptation is not only prevalent in the area of drinking. Thankfully, these principles can be applied to whatever temptation you may be dealing with. God has wisdom that is applicable to your present situation. I know people with all sorts of accountability partners—dating, financial, even exercise. God's Word is applicable no matter what situation you are in.

Accountability is essential even if you think you are not struggling. Not only because it is in the Bible, but also because we need to take precautionary measures toward our sin. Fellas, accountability in our sexual purity is a must. It does not matter if you are a virgin, a porn addict, or somewhere in between. You only have to take a glance at the latest movie trailer to figure our world is going to challenge our integrity. Find accountability, no matter what season of life you are in. Those without accountability long for it. Those held accountable are forever grateful.

> *Therefore, confess your sins to one another and pray for*
> *one another, that you may be healed.*
> —James 5:16

For an in-depth look on accountability, I highly recommend "Prayer Coach" by James L. Nicodem. Chapter 13 has some wonderful insights.

Don't Fall For The Devil's Trap

You do not have to go farther than your TV to discover the effects of alcohol. Just recall a movie scene when someone is drinking. Does that scene ever convey positive life change as a result? Not even biblically speaking. Even from a worldly standpoint, I would argue that alcohol is rarely portrayed in a positive context. Yet, why do so many continue to run towards it as if it will solve all their problems? The devil is one sly goose. When he tried to tempt Jesus in the desert, he was all about the short-term benefits. He's using the same method today in an effort to lure you into his scheme.

Doesn't Satan's method of luring appear dangerously familiar to how alcohol companies present their products? What do you see on Budweiser, Heineken, Smirnoff, and Captain Morgan commercials? Beautiful women and sharply dressed men who seem to be living the life. At best you will see a snippet of their night. They seem to be happy. They seem to be successful. But the scenes I see in commercials and the ones I see in real life do not seem to match up. The potential consequences seem greater than the rewards.

Isn't it also funny how these commercials seem to target youth more than regular, of-age drinkers? You never see ugly people in these commercials. You see young, fit, attractive guys and gals, the type of people many in our world strive to be like. Alcohol companies spend approximately $2 billion annually on advertising in the United States.[xii] As a young adult, you are the most influential and biggest potential customer of these companies. They know that if they can get you hooked on their products at a young age, they most likely have you for life. They couldn't care less about you. They just want your money. Why would you want to play their game? Why would you let anything hold you back during one of the most influential periods of your life?

Hell hates you. The devil is terrified of your potential influence. He is trying to trip you up and prevent you from using your influence. The world's portrayal of alcohol is one of his kamikazes against your generation. Keep your guard up, my friend.

Relationship vs. Religion

We have talked about a lot of do's and don'ts. It would be easy to think the narrow road is about following a list of rules. But I want us to remember and trust that all of His commandments are a gift for our benefit (John 10:10).

Let's bring it back to focus. What's the essence of a relationship with God? Trust. Think about a relationship you share with a close friend. I bet you would trust that person when he or she tells you something. You would trust your friend loves you and desires only what is best for you. How much more is this true with a holy, perfect, and infinite God?

It is so easy to lose focus. When life gets difficult, it is easy to slip into thinking that we know what is best for us. It becomes easy to think that we are missing out on something by taking the narrow road. However, God is not a Heavenly being who is trying to suck the joy out of our lives. Scripture is filled with passages about His love for us and how He relentlessly pursues us. He did not have to send His son to be butchered on the cross for our mistakes. He did not have to give us His Word to guide us to Him. But He did, and His son, Christ Jesus, is proof of His grace.

Jesus' words in John 10:10 forever changed my perspective on Scripture. Our Lord proclaims that unlike the devil, He has come to give us life in all of its abundance. Therefore, when He tells us not to do something (as we have seen a lot this chapter), He is not trying to make us miserable. He is simply saying, *"Derek, your life on earth would be the most fulfilling if you did not get drunk."* Or, *"D. Kim, your life on earth would bring me the most glory if you waited until marriage to have sex."* The list is endless. You fill in the blank. God's commandments are ultimately for our benefit! How ironic that sometimes we mislead ourselves into thinking we know our lives better than the One who created life itself!

Happiness is not God's main goal for us. Being completely satisfied in His beauty, splendor, majesty—Himself—is.

There have been times in my life where I have mistakenly put happiness before God. But what good is happiness if we remain dead in our sins (Matthew 16:26)? I am not saying God wants us to be depressed for the rest of our lives. God's Word brings us into knowledge of Him, which results in an overflowing wellspring of joy. It would be blasphemous to say all He wants is for you to feel good about yourself. For our periods of happiness are dung in comparison to personally knowing Him (Philippians 3:8). Again, it is not about what we want to hear but what we need to hear.

The greatest pleasure God could offer is Himself. The Bible is a love letter, not a rulebook. It would be so easy to become legalistic after a chapter like this. But let us not lose focus of the loving Shepherd who desires to guide us into green pastures and quiet waters (Psalm 23:2). He not only knows what is best for us, but He *is* what is best for us (2 Peter 1:3)! Focus exclusively on Him as you navigate the treacherous temptations of this world (Hebrews 12:2).

> *"Finally, be strong in the Lord and in the strength of His might."*
> —Ephesians 6:10

A Concerning Misconception

Aren't misconceptions the worst? Isn't it frustrating when people draw false conclusions by taking things out of context? I find this happens often with the things Jesus said. Out of every misconception or assumption I have encountered, let me tell you about the one I found most concerning.

Believe it or not, I had a friend who would tell me that he drank because it made him more like Jesus.

You can only imagine how confused I was when I heard something like this. For the sake of our conversation, we will call him Patrick. Prior to embarking on his senior spring break, Patrick explained to me how John 2:1-12 would be the justification for his upcoming actions in Mexico. I loved Patrick. He was known as a funny guy. But this time he had outdone himself.

The story of Jesus turning water into wine has to be one of the most popular stories among high school students. Not because of Jesus' first miracle, but because the event is commonly interpreted as an excuse for alcohol consumption. Once I returned from spring break, I eventually realized Patrick was not the only one with this mindset. In fact, I came to find this kind of thinking was quite common! I want to address a concerning misconception commonly associated with Jesus' miracle at the wedding of Cana. The problem has to do with taking Scripture out of context. There is frightening potential for universal justification when a verse is taken out of its original context. When people would come to such a conclusion after reading John 2:1-12, they make a mistake I have often made.

Taking Scripture out of context is a terrifying notion because it quickly leads to the justification of sin. You can end up justifying just about anything. You could justify so-called homosexual marriage. You could justify polygamy. You could justify premarital sex. The scary thing is people actually have rationalized all these ideas with Scripture. Therefore, I hope you see the importance of context. I would argue it is a matter of life and death.

I was introduced to a concept my junior year that changed the way I read the Bible: interpreting Scripture in its original first century, Jewish context. I'm not saying we need to become Bible scholars to completely understand Scripture. However, we must study God's Word in lights of its original framework. We must remember, as foolish as it may sound, Biblical accounts did not occur in 21st century, American culture. Context changes everything. Have you ever heard someone say something about the Bible that seemed a little fishy? Better yet, have you heard people take one or two verses and build an entire theology around them? False teachers and cults have been doing this for centuries. The scary problem is if you take an idea out of its original context, you are not seeing the passage through its proper lens. It is like if I were to interpret the historicity of the South African Apartheid with the traditions of Canadian Boxing day. Needless to say, I would make false assumptions and come to faulty conclusions. We are all guilty of butchering Scripture. There have been times I have used the Word of God as a crutch to make me feel better instead of letting it be the ultimate authority of my life.

The events of Scripture occurred in first century, Jewish culture. If you read the Old Testament, you might find some of God's commandments to the Israelites pretty weird. Don't let cattle graze with other types of cattle, don't wear clothes with two different materials... what's all this about (Leviticus 19:19)? As strange as these commandments may seem, God's commandments make complete sense in the context of the Exodus. As a chosen nation, Israel was not to pervert itself with surrounding pagan communities who were not held to the same standards as they were. Even in something as small as the clothes they wore, they were to observe the magnitude of God's holiness and the sacredness of His commandments. In other words, the Israelites were commanded to pursue holiness, just like we are commanded to pursue holiness.

Therefore, it would be a misunderstanding to interpret Scripture from a 21st century, American context as we so often do. Because of the first century, Jewish context of Scripture, we must be wary of interpreting Jesus' miracle of turning water into wine as a justification for alcohol abuse.

So lets get back to Patrick's theory. Observing the story from its original context, what can we learn from Jesus' miracle in John 2:1-12?

Jesus is a Supernatural Creator. You would not have wanted to be the bridegroom at this wedding. A significant part of ancient Near East weddings was wine during the wedding feast.[xiii] If wine ran out, the bridegroom and his family could be liable for paying for the inadequacy.[xiv] Wine was not cheap, even though this was 2000 years ago! But when things seem to be going downhill, Jesus shows He is a graceful creator and provider. He commands the servants to fill the jars with water and performs the first miracle of His earthly ministry. Jesus shows grace in a particularly desperate situation, foreshadowing His ultimate provision and sacrifice that is to come at the cross of Calvary.

Jesus is the Messiah. I have learned to pay close attention to detail when reading Scripture. One of the beauties of the Bible is how the New Testament complements the Old Testament and vice-versa. Always remember, the best complement for the Bible is the Bible. In the Old Testament, Amos prophesized an abundance of wine with the coming of the Messiah. Therefore, as His first miracle, Jesus was making a bold statement. He was claiming He was the Messiah, the Anointed One who would restore Israel to glory. This was a big deal. It had been prophesized of for hundreds of years. It prompted an immediate reaction from people. There was no middle ground. It was the reason Jesus was eventually crucified. There are things in the Bible that should be taken literally and others symbolically. Here is an instance of how the symbolism of wine holds a far greater connotation not only for those at the wedding, but also for the rest of humanity!

Bible commentaries are phenomenal tools to help you learn the context of Scripture. Once I downloaded John MacArthur's Bible Commentary on my iPad, I couldn't believe what I had been missing out on! The expertise of authors like John MacArthur has helped me to understand the Bible on a deeper level. Check out your local bookstore, or ask your pastor to see if he can hook you up. Be sure to check out other resources such as topical indexes, accordances, and Bible maps, which will shed further light on the historicity of Scripture.

Context not only presents the proper framework behind the Bible, but also brings Scripture to life. Yes, Jesus is the vine and we are the branches, but did you know this was the last thing He said to His disciples before He was crucified? Yes, Jesus has a plan for your life as he said in Jeremiah 29:11, but are you aware the people who heard this promise were exiled in a foreign land for 70 years and didn't live to see the promise fulfilled? Yes, Jesus gives us the strength to do all things, but did you know Philippians 4:13 is more about contentment than scoring touchdowns and acing exams you never studied for?

I hope you understand the seriousness behind this concept. Nitpicking verses and twisting them according to our means robs Scripture of its objectivity. Jesus turning water into wine has nothing to do with high school binge drinking. I would even argue wine is rarely presented in positive context throughout Scripture[3]. Jesus' first miracle is not an excuse to drink. If that is your interpretation, then you are missing out on the abundant insight the story provides in its proper context. May we be wise as serpents, innocent as doves, quick to listen, and slow to speak (Matthew 10:16, James 1:19).

Jesus, The All-Satisfying Savior.

Some might think this is a radical stance. You are entitled to your opinion. However, it would break my heart to watch a generation neglect its opportunity to influence others for Christ. If something as frivolous as a drink in a glass has the potential to ruin the potential of young men and women, only a response the world deems as radical would be appropriate. Your influence matters. There is power in your presence.

As you enter into a hostile environment, you need to figure out

your true motivation for fighting against temptation. What is your foundation? Are you really trusting in what God says or do you think good morals are enough? Do you have faith that God truly wants what is best for you, or do you think you have a better grasp on your life? God's promises are the only foundation that will withstand the heaviest storms. Our minds are curious and will tempt us toward a place we do not want to go. Temptation will bombard you from every direction. Hell is going to try to take you down. But let us take hope; having faith that Jesus is worth infinitely more than any temptation of Hades. Your generation has great potential. So why give the devil any sort of foothold in your life (Eph. 4:26-27)? Jesus is the only One who satisfies. May we find fulfillment in Him alone.

> "We are half-hearted creatures, fooling about with drink and sex and ambition when infinite joy is offered us, like an ignorant child who wants to go on making mud pies in a slum because he cannot imagine what is meant by the offer of a holiday at the sea. We are far too easily pleased."
> —C.S. Lewis

> *Oh, taste and see that the LORD is good! Blessed is the man who takes refuge in him!*
> —Psalm 34:8

Chapter Eight
Year Three: Junior Year

Therefore, preparing your minds for action, and being sober-minded, set your hope fully on the grace that will be brought to you at the revelation of Jesus Christ.
—1 Peter 1:13

Can you believe you are finally an upperclassmen? Gone are the days of getting trampled in the halls and not having a seat at lunch. Hooray! But Junior year is infamously known for its standardized testing and advanced placement classes. Along with academic pursuits, eleventh grade is also the crucial year in the recruiting process for potential collegiate athletes. Talk about pressure. The plethora of demands can be overwhelming. That is, if you take your eyes off of the One who got you this far in the first place.

Not that I have already obtained this or am already perfect, but I press on to make it my own, because Christ Jesus has made me his own. Brothers, I do not consider that I have made it my own. But one thing I do: forgetting what lies behind and straining forward to what lies ahead, I press on toward the goal for the prize of the upward call of God in Christ Jesus.
—Philippians 3:12-14

Junior year is no walk in the park. In fact, if I had to decide which year was the hardest, it would be my junior year—no question. However, if you asked me to choose the year I grew the most out of my four years, my answer would remain the same. It's funny, because my most sincere prayer as a junior was that I would grow stronger in my faith. I quickly discovered that praying for growth is equivalent to praying for trials. This is not a new concept. Whether it is muscle mass or our personal sanctification, you always tear something down before building it back up.

The Lord promptly answered my request for spiritual growth. As the weeks and months flew by, there were more parties, more heckling from my peers, and more purity vows broken by my friends than any year before. I increasingly felt as though I was the only Christian in my entire school. It was this year when Matthew 7:13-14 spoke to me the loudest. I realized that Jesus was not looking for half-hearted followers. I had to stand firm in what I believed in. Not just as a follower of Jesus Christ, but also in the effort I put into my studies and on the playing field. As I was challenged spiritually, academically, and the athletically, I was forced to make a decision similar to that of David's as a young boy: was I going to stare at the size of my giants or marvel at the size of my God?

If you want to grow into the young man or woman God has destined you to be, you must be willing to take on the challenges. It is time to step your game up. With college and scholarship applications just around the corner, get on that study grind so you can present yourself as the best candidate possible. This goes for athletics too. You want to work your butt off in the weight room, in the pool, or on the court so when the season is over, you are not ashamed of the highlight film you are sending out to prospective schools. You don't want to look back on a year like this with any kinds of regrets.

More than ever, fellowship is crucial. Remember to surround yourselves with heart and soul brothers and sisters who are going to stir you onto love and good deeds. Most importantly, never disregard fellowship with your Heavenly Father, as he prepares to do some major

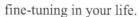

fine-tuning in your life.

Adversity is the greatest opportunity. The finest steels are made in the hottest of fires. So prepare your minds for action. Take heart, and tackle this year head-on with the confidence that comes from keeping your eyes on the "*faithful God who keeps covenant and steadfast love with those who love him and (keeps) his commandments, to a thousand generations,*" (Deuteronomy 7:9). No matter what happens, find comfort in the fact that "*Jesus Christ is the same yesterday and today and forever*" (Hebrews 13:8). Don't give up. You are almost done!

> *And I am sure of this, that he who began a good work in you will bring it to completion at the day of Jesus Christ.*
> —Philippians 1:6

Chapter Nine
The Narrow Road Through Dating

For this is the will of God, your sanctification: that you abstain from sexual immorality; that each one of you know how to control his own body in holiness and honor, not in the passion of lust like the Gentiles who do not know God.
—1 Thessalonians 4:3-5

So flee youthful passions and pursue righteousness, faith, love and peace, along with those who call on the Lord from a pure heart.
—2 Timothy 2:22

The Truth About Love

Isn't it funny how we used to be terrified of the opposite gender? In high school, the days of cooties have faded away; you encounter a new obstacle—a misconception of boyfriends, girlfriends, sex, and what love truly is.

How many girls did I date in high school, you ask? The same number of outright national championships the University of Michigan has in football since 1948. Zero. You are not going to be hearing from a dating expert. I cannot speak as authoritatively on this matter as I would like. Hence, I plan to emphasize Biblical truth—the ultimate authority—over personal experience, to help you realize the significance of intimacy between a man and a woman.

Singleness gave me a unique perspective on relationships; it is not the curse the world portrays it to be, as we will soon discover. In fact, the Bible calls it a blessing. In this chapter, we are not only going to talk about dating, but also relationships in general. I have a special treat for you at the end, a subchapter discussing one of the most powerful forces in the universe. It is essential you hear what God has to say about these matters, because you will hear quite the opposite at the lunch table, in the locker room, and in pop culture.

Why Do You Want A Boyfriend Or Girlfriend?

It is not a bad thing to want be loved. It is natural to desire intimacy with someone of the opposite sex. Our emotions are what make us human. God displays emotion throughout the Bible. He shows compassion as well as wrath while leading the Israelites to the Promised Land. Jesus wept, rejoiced, and flipped tables out of anger during His earthly ministry. We are made in God's image, and it is no question our emotions are a crucial part of our existence.

But sometimes we let our emotions get the best of us.

The journey to the Promised Land was not easy. Can you imagine wandering in a desert for 40 years? *"Would it not be better for us to go back to Egypt?"* the Israelites groaned (Numbers 14:3). They let their present affliction become the authority for their way of thinking. What if Jesus' decisions were dictated by his emotions? Hanging on a plank of torture while being mocked and spit upon, He easily could have ended the anguish by calling down angels from Heaven. But to Jesus, God's eternal purpose took precedence over His temporary emotion.

Emotions are excellent indicators, but terrible motivators.

I am sure you can recall a time when your feelings motivated you to do something you regret. Emotions will play a part in our

decision-making; however, our conduct must primarily be rooted in truth, revealed in the person of Jesus Christ through His Word.

So how does this relate to dating? Too often, emotions become the driving force in a relationship. She is cute. He is charming. She is everything you have ever wanted. He meets all your criteria. Meanwhile, Jesus takes a backseat. We were built with a desire for love—a God shaped hole. However, we often try to fill a God-shaped hole with humanistic pieces. We seek affection in all the wrong places. People make terrible substitutions for God. People are meant to encourage us on our journey; they were never meant to be the foundation of our joy. That is God's rightful place. He wants to be our first love.

Before we can experience love with another imperfect human being, we must first experience God, because God is love (1 John 4:8). So here is the question: have you forgotten (or never experienced) your first love?

> *But I have this against you, that you have abandoned the love you had at first. Remember therefore from where you have fallen; repent, and do the works you did at first. If not, I will come to you and remove your lampstand from its place, unless you repent.*
> —Revelation 2:4-5

Pause. If you are not yet a follower of Christ, and have never experienced God's perfect love, then I encourage you to flip to the "Good News" chapter before venturing further. Only supernatural affection satisfies the longing of the human soul. All love flows from Jesus. And where we seek love is often our greatest blunder. It is a tragic mistake to look for fulfillment in another sinful human being.

Brother or sister, if you have been ignoring Jesus' perfect love, and trying to satisfy your longings through a dating relationship, you have two options: the wide, easy road that "feels good" and is popular, or God's narrow road of repentance. The original Greek word for "repent" means to do a 180-degree turn. It is the idea that you completely turn from the wide road you were on, and sprint in the other direction. We can

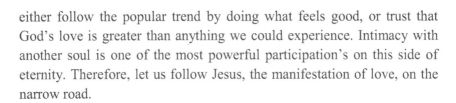

either follow the popular trend by doing what feels good, or trust that God's love is greater than anything we could experience. Intimacy with another soul is one of the most powerful participation's on this side of eternity. Therefore, let us follow Jesus, the manifestation of love, on the narrow road.

> *Your steadfast love, O LORD, extends to the heavens,*
> *your faithfulness to the clouds.*
> —Psalm 36:5

> *Because your steadfast love is better than life, my lips*
> *will praise you.*
> —Psalm 63:3

The Purpose of Dating

Do you feel pressure to be in a relationship? I know I do.

"Colin and Aubrey are the perfect match for each other."

"Joe and Lauren look so happy when I stalk their Facebook pictures" (Admit it, we have all done it!)

"Did you hear how Aaron asked Sarah to Homecoming?" "Oh wait! Your best friend just got asked as well!"

And you? Well, you are more concerned with the type of ice cream you will be eating Friday night rather than finding a date to the big dance.

Pop culture also adds to the pressure. Every song is about how *"I want you back"* or *"Why you belong with me."* Movies say the only way to be content is by having Prince Charming or Cinderella at your side.

But have you ever asked yourself what the purpose of dating really is?

Just like anything else, if you do not know a task's purpose, you are unlikely to perform it effectively. Moreover, not knowing the overall objective will end up causing more harm than good. And how much more careful should we be when dealing with the deepest, most sensitive parts of our being?

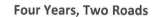

Before we go any further, we need to define the purpose of dating—the question our culture often skips. It is time that we stop playing games, and start being intentional. What is the purpose of this phenomenon?

To find the person you want to marry and spend the rest of your life with.

And how can dating be defined?

Spending time with a specific person whom you believe has the qualities and character traits you desire in your future spouse.

Simply put, the end purpose of dating is marriage. So when you ask, *"May I have the privilege of being your boyfriend?"* or reply *"Yes, I would love to be your girlfriend"* you are sending a powerful message. It's more like, *"I believe I'm the person you could spend the rest of your life with."* or *"Yes, you have the qualities I seek in a future husband."*

Are you beginning to see how powerful these relationships are?

Dating is not just about making each other happy; dating is about an eternal bond that reflects a sacred image: Christ and His church. Let us pledge to value the true purpose and definition of dating—truth over trend. The consequences of misunderstanding this topic are severe. Because if dating is a predecessor to marriage, then our interactions with our boyfriend or girlfriend influence how we will view our future spouse.

Now, let us look at the bigger picture. If dating is about marriage, and marriage is about Jesus and His church, then what does this look like?

Jesus + Church = Marriage

"Whoa, Derek, isn't marriage something old people think about?" High school is a paradox in this matter. On one hand, part of you is eager to find that special someone. On the other hand, the days of proposals and in-laws seem a century away. But you must understand

what you are getting yourself into. Again, without purpose, we will be tossed and turned by every opinion that reaches our ears.

My message is not that high school dating is necessarily bad, but that most students have no idea what they are getting themselves into, which causes a lot of bad. Isn't this proven by the unnecessary drama and broken friendships that derive from a breakup? The separation often results in heartbreak and long-term emotional wounds. So, no, marriage is not something only old people should think about. Matrimony should be in the back of your mind, because chances are that you will develop feelings for someone in the near future, and you need to know how to respond. The Bible is clear that marriage is not a mundane phenomenon. The relationship between a man and a woman is one of God's most powerful platforms to display His Gospel.

When reading through the Bible, you realize that God is not only worthy of glory, but that He demands it. Beginning in Genesis 1:27 we see that men and women were made in His image, to reflect His splendor. In the Exodus, God's glory engulfs Mt. Sinai; no man could lay a finger on the mountain and live.

Fast forward to the Gospel accounts, where God comes down in human flesh through His son Jesus Christ. The Son of God, born in a feeding trough, goes on to walk on water, heal the sick, and defeat sin and death once and for all. Paul's letters continue the theme of God's glory. A former murderer of Christians, Paul exclaims in 1 Corinthians 10:13 how all is to be accomplished for the glory of God—even something as mundane as eating and drinking. Furthermore, he explains in Colossians 1:16-17 how *all things were created through him and for him ... he is before all things and in him all things hold together.*

Not only is everything in existence meant to glorify God, but He is also the one holding the cosmos, the Amazon Jungle, and every mitochondria in our body together. Finally, in John's Revelation, we gaze at the final outcome. Jesus receives the glory He deserves. Satan is defeated. No more tears. No more pain. No more death. The glory of God replaces the sun, and believers worship Him for the rest of endless time.

Therefore, if God's story is all about His glory, then how much more should He be magnified in the union of a man and a woman—the

pinnacle of His creation work?

As Paul explains in Ephesians 5:22-33, marriage is meant to be the ultimate representation of Jesus' love for His church.

> *Wives, submit to your own husbands as to the Lord. For the husband is the head of the wife even as Christ is the head of the church, his body, and is himself its Savior. Now as the church submits to Christ, so also wives should submit in everything to their husbands. Husbands, love your wives, as Christ loved the church and gave himself up for her, that he might sanctify her, having cleansed her by the washing of water with the word, so that he might present the church to himself in splendor, without spot or wrinkle or any such thing, that she might be holy and without blemish. In the same way husbands should love their wives as their own bodies. He who loves his wife loves himself. For no one ever hated his own flesh, but nourishes and cherishes it, just as Christ does the church, because we are members of his body. "Therefore a man shall leave his father and mother and hold fast to his wife, and the two shall become one flesh." This mystery is profound, and I am saying that it refers to Christ and the church. However, let each one of you love his wife as himself, and let the wife see that she respects her husband.*
> —Ephesians 5:22-33

You want to know about romance? Be awed by Christ's pursuit of His church. This is where the concept of marriage and, in turn, dating, stems from. He demonstrates His love for her by pursuing her, sanctifying her, and laying down His life for her. For this reason, it is not enough for Jesus to be a compartment in our relationships. Jesus cannot merely be first; He must be everything. Jesus must be the center because *"in him all things hold together."*

Is it possible to date at your age and bring God glory? Perhaps.

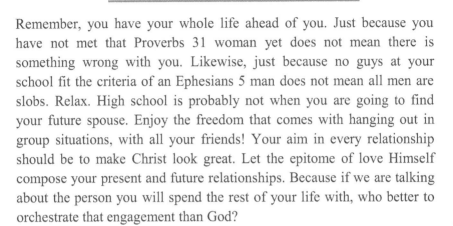

Remember, you have your whole life ahead of you. Just because you have not met that Proverbs 31 woman yet does not mean there is something wrong with you. Likewise, just because no guys at your school fit the criteria of an Ephesians 5 man does not mean all men are slobs. Relax. High school is probably not when you are going to find your future spouse. Enjoy the freedom that comes with hanging out in group situations, with all your friends! Your aim in every relationship should be to make Christ look great. Let the epitome of love Himself compose your present and future relationships. Because if we are talking about the person you will spend the rest of your life with, who better to orchestrate that engagement than God?

Reality Check

Reality TV is anything but reality. Much like Jersey Shore is a skewed representation of life on the East Coast, our minds and emotions are clouded by a distorted reality when we think we have found that special someone.

We've all witnessed the two lovebirds at school. Their entire schedules revolve around each other. They study together, eat lunch together, text until 4 a.m., and are practically attached at the hip in the hallways. Not to mention the public display of affection at their lockers —which also somehow ended up next to each other.

Reality check.

Okay, so maybe you haven't drifted that far into lala land. However, it is hard to deny that when you are interested in someone, you get tempted to do things for him or her you would not do for anyone else. Isn't it wild the extent people will go to for someone or something they love?

Remember, emotions are not a bad thing. But without the Spirit's discernment, passion can lead us down a haphazard road of regret. Emotion is a pillar, not a cornerstone. Falling into false reality will only develop destructive tendencies for the future. Even when you are married, your fulfillment and worth should not come from your spouse. True love stems from abiding in reality—truth—Jesus.

Reality Check #1: Two Outcomes

One of two things are going to happen to your relationship:

1. You break up.
2. You get married.

It does not really hit you at first. When you are "head over heels" for someone, you don't consider the risks involved, or you tell yourself that "this one is different." But in reality, it's either the marriage altar or an eventual memory.

Reality Check #2: God's Standard

You should have high standards for your future boyfriend or girlfriend. Good hygiene, respectful to your parents, covers their mouth when they sneeze. All of these are commendable; however, God has one ultimate standard:

> *...She is free to be married to whom she wishes, only in the Lord.*
> —1 Corinthians 7:39

> *Do not be unequally yoked with unbelievers. For what partnership has righteousness with lawlessness? Or what fellowship has light with darkness?*
> —2 Corinthians 6:14

These verses are not referring to whom you sit next to at lunch. Paul's letters to the Corinthian church are not saying that we are forbidden from having non-Christian friends. He is talking about a more serious issue. Dating is a whole other category because of its extraordinary purpose and definition—to find the person we want to spend the rest of our life with, and spending time with someone whom we believe has the qualities we yearn for in a spouse. Or, as Genesis 2:24 puts it, the person we will eventually become "one flesh" with.

To some extent, this commandment might sound legalistic, but remember that God only tells us things that are good for us. God's commandments are rooted in His love. Think about a parent-child relationship. When a dad sets limits for his child, or when a mom says "NO!" they are not trying to make their children miserable. Instead, a parent's guidance is meant to protect and provide the best opportunities for the child. How much more does this apply to a Heavenly Father and His children?

The Bible calls us to marry and date believers—period.

For some, this is the toughest pill to swallow. However, this is not an obscure commandment in the Old or New Testament. In Deuteronomy, God commanded Israel to not wed those of pagan nations. God's people were meant to be holy—set apart for a specific purpose. Our relationships are not supposed to look like the world's relationships, not because we are better, but because we are called to be holy as our God is holy (1 Peter 1:16).

This brings up the topic of missionary dating, also popularly known as "flirt to convert".

"I know they are not a believer, but I am witnessing to them."

"He is so close to accepting Christ."

"She comes from a church background; she just needs a little time."

May I be frank? It is not going to work. It is not Biblical. It is not pleasing to God.

This concept of missionary dating can be compared to playing tug-of-war on a hill. The Christian boy, who is on top of the hill, tries with all his might to pull his beloved unbelieving girlfriend, to knowledge of the truth. He brings her to youth group, buys her a Bible, even texts her verses in the morning. These acts are not bad in and of themselves, but in the end they are futile because they are not accomplished in the appropriate context. In a spiritual game of tug-of-war, the person on the top is always going to lose. The burden of an unregenerate heart is just too great.

I found that missionary dating was one of the most common mistakes made by my fellow brothers and sisters in Christ. However, if Jesus is whom marriage is modeled after, it only makes sense that the relationship revolves around Him—on both sides.

As we will talk about next, it all boils down to motive. Are you attracted to her because of her relationship with Christ? Or is she just someone who makes your heart beat faster? When searching for a soul mate, it's not about looking for a "good person." Nor should you seek someone who is religious. Don't search for someone who will just go to church with you. Your standard should be God's eternal standard: someone who is in love with Jesus Christ. Salvation should never be a question. This is an area of no compromise.

Reality #3: True Motive

Pride usually tells us our motives are clean. And it is easy to compare yourself to others, isn't it? *"We both go to church, unlike so-and-so." "At least we are not hook up partners like them."* Additionally, there is a plethora of underlying motivations.

- *"Everyone else has a boyfriend or girlfriend."*
- *"People are making fun of me because I am a virgin."*
- *"I don't like being known for being prude"*
- *"That girl or guy is hot. It is only natural to follow physical attraction, right?"*

Prayer and meditation on God's Word are mediums through which you become aware of your true movies. Get alone, put the phone away, drop to your knees with your Bible, and seek the subtle voice of the Holy Spirit. We only harm ourselves if we are not honest.

Jack, my youth pastor, would tell a story of how his oldest son would always hide in the same spot during hide-and-seek. The funny thing was that Luke always thought he had his dad beat. *"You'll never find me!"* he yelled. Don't we tend to do the same with God?

> *The eyes of the LORD are in every place, keeping watch*
> *on the evil and the good.*
> —Proverbs 15:3

We are talking about the eyes that saw creation come into being and knows the number of hairs on our heads. Therefore, it is foolish to think that He doesn't know our motives. King David understood the

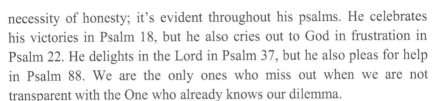

necessity of honesty; it's evident throughout his psalms. He celebrates his victories in Psalm 18, but he also cries out to God in frustration in Psalm 22. He delights in the Lord in Psalm 37, but he also pleas for help in Psalm 88. We are the only ones who miss out when we are not transparent with the One who already knows our dilemma.

We need to ask ourselves, "Is the purpose of this relationship to glorify Jesus OR is there another notion to our affections?"

> *"Even before a word is on my tongue, behold, O LORD,*
> *you know it all together"*
> —Psalm 139:4

Dynamic Duo

One might be the loneliest number, but do not underestimate the number two. Many things in life come in duos: gloves, lungs, skis, and a man and a woman in love. While there are many aspects to a God-honoring relationship, I believe it boils down to two things: Jesus and integrity. The latter is a result of the former.

First, Jesus cannot be a part of the relationship. You heard me correctly. Jesus is not just something you two should have in common. Jesus is not an appetizer to the full meal. No. Jesus *is* the relationship. In Scripture, everything is about Jesus. From Moses to Macedonia, from morning to evening, from man's first breath in Genesis to the celestial roars of the redeemed in Revelation, Jesus has, does, and will hold everything together.

If you've checked your motives, feelings, and standards, and you decide to pursue a relationship with someone else who is "in Christ," then Christ should be the center of it all. There is not a more appropriate time to be a Jesus freak, or *freaks* I should say. Read through the New Testament together. Pray over one another. Immerse yourselves in fellowship. Serve in the children's ministry side-by-side. Fight the good fight together. Ask other believers to keep you accountable on sexual purity and how much time you spend with one another. Accountability is a crucial component of a healthy marriage. Therefore, as preparation for marriage, dating couples must also learn to display transparency, so that they are openly held to God's standard of integrity.

Here is another paradox: Do not focus on each other. Because if the core of the relationship is to satisfy one another's needs, you are going to completely miss the point.

I like to compare this concept with my first international mission trip. I still remember my first thoughts walking into the first team meeting.

"Crap."

"I am going to be stuck with these clowns for a week?"

"I have to room with him?"

"I have to spend three hours on a bus with her?"

Now, understand that I had no animosity toward my brothers and sisters. It was simply the realization that on this trip, I would be spending time with people I wouldn't usually hang out with. But guess what happened when we got back? I said to myself, "Wow, I actually kind of miss that guy! ...I did not even know her before this trip, but now it feels like I have known her for years!"

But we did not get together at the beginning of the week and say, *"hey, let's all be friends!"* No! We were 30 people on one mission. And as we pursued Christ's mission, He knit unity amongst the people who were on His mission.

All the more is this true in a dating relationship. It is only through pursuing Christ that everything works out the way it is supposed to. " *... in Him that all things hold together"* (Colossians 1:17). If you both focus on loving Jesus, you will not have to think about loving each other. If you are both obeying God's Word, there will be a couple mistakes here and there, but the majority of your conduct will be the natural overflow of a delight in the Lord. When two believers strive together, God orchestrates their lives according to His will.

> *But seek first the kingdom of God and his righteousness,*
> *and all these things will be added to you.*
> —Matthew 6:33

*For by him all things were created, in heaven and on
earth, visible and invisible, whether thrones or
dominions or rulers or authorities—all things were
created through him and for him. And he is before all
things, and in him all things hold together.*
—Colossians 1:16-17

Second, establish boundaries. Establishing physical and emotional
boundaries should be one of the first things a couple does. The time to
strategize for a battle is not as you approach the front lines; it's
beforehand. Victory is established through strategic preparation.
Complacency leads to trouble. Boundaries protect us from the
deceitfulness of our hormones and also communicate faith. Trust is
pivotal. And when a couple establishes boundaries, they distinguish
integrity from temporary, sensual fulfillment. Selflessness resounds from
that message—a loud statement of love and character—attributes
prevalent in a God-fearing future spouse.

Vow not to put yourself in compromising situations. In King
David's lamentable episode with Bathsheba, his first mistake was not
when he told Joab, "Send me Uriah the Hittite." It was when he put
himself in a situation where he could be tempted. In first century Jewish
society, the roof was a common location for bathing. Thus, when David
was strolling on his rooftop during the evening, he was walking in a
setting that could challenge his integrity. He put himself in a
compromising situation, which was his first mistake. When David saw
Bathsheba bathing, he could have looked away, but he let his hormones
get the best of him. He glanced at temptation a second time, another
mistake. Before he knew it, the powerful tug of sexual temptation
spurred him to make more decisions contradictory to God's Word. His
adultery with Bathsheba was not his sole failure. Rather, the battle was
lost in the decisions he made up to that point.

Watching a movie lying on his bed, when his parents aren't
home, is probably not the best idea. That's putting yourself into a
compromising situation. The flirting gets a little too physical, and before

you both know it, you're in a tickle fight with each other. That's choosing temptation a second time. You must nip sexual temptation in the bud, before it's too late.

Consider double dates. Stay in public as much as you can when out and about. There's nothing wrong with some alone time. But be intentional and wise about your whereabouts, knowing that one look of the eyes, or one touch too far up the legs, is more than enough to set off the wildfire of immorality. And once the blaze starts, it's almost impossible to stop. The flesh is too weak.

Set the boundary at kissing. The Bible may not specifically state a boundary for dating couples. However, the severity of sexual immorality is a monumental theme. For some, kissing might even be too much. If it turns you on too much, don't even go there. It just isn't worth the risk. You are going to have to be honest with each other. With Christ at the crux of the relationship, you need to make the decision that best honors Him.

> *But sexual immorality and all impurity or covetousness must not even be named among you, as is proper among saints.*
> —Ephesians 5:3

Rumors? Mentions? Nope. Sexual sin should not even be a part of the conversation, as foreign as a Chick-fil-A in Michigan. Keep in mind; dating is not only about the physical aspect. Lets go back to the purpose: *to find the person you want to spend the rest of your life with.* So when dating someone—on the coffee dates, Skype sessions, and stargazing rendezvous—you are growing closer to one another in an effort to figure out if they are "the one." Now, when the affections drift into the realm of physical intimacy, an exclusive line is flirted with. A peck on the lips or holding hands while out on the town might be fine. However, when we start getting a little too touchy-feely, we cross into the realm reserved for a much deeper union.

So what is it about this unfamiliar realm of emotional boundaries? The problem I notice in relationships nowadays is not that they are actually dating, but instead playing marriage.

> *Keep your heart with all vigilance, for from it flow the*
> *springs of life.*
> —Proverbs 4:23

Playing marriage can cause problems. Emotional intimacy comes before physical intimacy. Yes, get to know one another. Discover each other's hopes, dreams, aspirations, and struggles. However, don't spill all the beans of your entire personal life in the first few dates. Consider this: whatever you tell him, whatever secret you share with her, he or she will know—forever. And you don't even know if this is going to last! Therefore, girls, encourage him to earn your favor. Fellas, respect the sensitive areas of her heart. Hold one another to a higher standard. You will never regret waiting, and the heart is one of the best investments. Contrary to popular belief, there is such thing as "moving too fast." Sleeping over at one another's house and hanging out to the point of sacrificing time with your other friends crosses over into that exclusive area. Being in love is one thing, but it's another thing to create a fantasy where all the benefits of a marriage are provided without the lifelong commitment.

If you choose to be in a relationship, be honest with yourself. Relationship idolatry is a pandemic among young adults. When Lifehouse's "Everything" comes on your iTunes and you hear, "*You're all I want, you're all I need, everything, everything,*"[xv] do those words describe your longing for him more than your longing for Jesus? Maybe "Two is Better than One" in some situations, but do Taylor Swift's lyrics, "*it's true I can't live without you,*"[xvi] better reflect your desire for God, or your yearning for another imperfect human being?

Single and Satisfied

Whatever predispositions you have about singleness, I want you to throw them out the window. Our perception of singleness is based more on what the world says than what the Bible says. We live in a culture where singleness is looked upon as a second-class status. That's not what the Bible says about being single. The Word of God says singleness is a *gift*—an exclusive opportunity for purposeful independence. We live in a world where contentment is far-fetched, and going to Homecoming alone is considered an abomination. But the last area we need discontentment is in intimacy with another soul. We know that the Bible has plenty to say about marriage. But does Scripture also address singles? You bet!

I want you to set this book down and turn to 1 Corinthians 7, particularly verses 25-35. There are a few things to keep in mind as you read this epistle. Paul here is addressing the Corinthian church on principles for marriage and singleness. Do you notice how he didn't leave anyone out of the conversation? Married people, divorced people, singles, widows, widowers, slaves, virgins, uncircumcised, circumcised —everyone plays a part in Jesus' church. Let's concentrate on verses 25-35, where Paul addresses singles. I see two conclusions we can draw from this passage.

First, singleness is *biblically* good. I think, in a sense, this part of Paul's letter is one big reality check to the Corinthians.

After the honeymoon, every marriage has its rough patches (just ask any married couple). Have you noticed that Hollywood never shows you life after the kiss in the pouring rain? Likewise, dating couples experience their ups and downs as well. When you are in a relationship with someone, you have to keep his or her needs in mind as well as your own. A boyfriend and a girlfriend need to make sure they are spending adequate time with one another. Couples have duties and concerns that are foreign to single persons (v. 32-35). A wife and a husband need to tend to the well being of their children. But, on the other hand, singles are free from such "anxieties"—they have more flexibility than their counterparts! And Paul is saying this flexibility isn't so you can play more Call of Duty or start another TV series on Netflix. As a single person, you have ample opportunity to make disciples and be His witnesses. Every Friday and Saturday night doesn't have to be spent with a boyfriend or girlfriend. Instead, you can use that time to build Gospel relationships with your classmates, teammates, or neighbors. That money you would have spent on a boyfriend or girlfriend's Christmas present, you can now give to support missionaries in the 10/40 Window, the area of the world that is home to the most unreached people groups and the least evangelized countries.

The Bible opens our eyes to the rich opportunities of singleness. This time in your life has a distinct purpose, and you can take advantage of it by being intentional. There is nothing wrong with being independent. The Bible is clear: Singleness is not a plague.

Second, singleness is meant to make God look great. Singleness and marriage both share an infinitely important purpose: to display the saving Gospel of Jesus Christ. The married couple portrays Christ's unconditional love for His church in a husband's sacrificial love for his wife. The woman's submission to her husband is a beautiful picture of the church's submission to Jesus, the church's head.

Singleness portrays the Gospel differently, yet still glorifies God. The single Christian portrays God's salvific endeavor by showing that his or her true identity is in Christ. True spiritual maturity has nothing to do with marital status. Human beings make terrible substitutions for God. The single person in Christ demonstrates that a husband or a wife is not necessary in order to have eternal satisfaction.

Lastly, the single person in Christ affirms the fact that God's people—the church—do not multiply through conception but by Holy Spirit regeneration. A woman's worth is not at all tied to the number of children she can have. Both men and women should find comfort that a husband or a wife is not necessary to advance God's Kingdom on earth. It is the Holy Spirit who gives life to the dead and sight to the blind, not any act of human will. You have freedom in Christ, Christian! You do not have to be entangled in the world's counterfeit standards of worth and identity! Christ is all in all, as Colossians 3:11 says. The love of God truly is *that* good.

I want to stress again that the Bible is in no way belittling marriage or the pursuit of marriage. You will see Paul emphasize this throughout 1 Corinthians 7. Singles and married couples both have exceptional opportunity to glorify God. And neither group is restricted in

114

spreading the Gospel. Every person has a unique purpose in the Kingdom of God. Marriage or relationship status should not hinder commitment to God. Simply put, every situation has its pros and cons.

I never had a high school sweetheart. The Lord graciously allowed me to take a few of His daughters to Homecoming and Prom. However, nothing resulted in a serious relationship. I'll admit I felt lonely at times. There were times I was tempted to find my worth in what girls said and thought about me. But looking back, I thank God that He used this time (and is still using it) to begin to teach me the secret of being content.

True contentment does not waver. From your first date to your wedding night and throughout your potential marriage, the more content you are in Christ, the freer you will be. And as a single person who is free from the dedication to a partner, you are in an ideal circumstance to discover a truth that will forever change your life.

Finding fulfillment in a boyfriend, girlfriend, or any other human being is one of the most hateful things you could do. Because when you trust someone to mimic God in your life, joy becomes a cruel parody. You hold him or her to a standard that is impossible to keep.

Married, single, it does not matter. We should never find our identity in people. Our contentment ought never to cease to overflow from Jesus Christ our Lord. And much like Christ, contentment does not change with our circumstances. That is why Paul proclaims in Philippians 4:13 that he can do all things through Him who gives him strength. Not to feel better about himself. Not to score more touchdowns. Not so he could ace a test he didn't study for. But so that whatever life throws at him, he can be fulfilled in Jesus, only Jesus.

Does this mean you have to be single for the rest of your life? Not necessarily. We can trust the amazing promise of Romans 8:28. Relax. You have the rest of your life ahead of you. There is no need to panic because you are not in love at 15, 16, 17, or 18 years old. High school is not usually when most people find their life partner (despite what Hollywood and High School Musical would have you believe!). There are many other pursuits worth your time and dedication.

You have one everlasting pursuit: Jesus. As you strive toward the eternal prize, occasionally look to your left and look to your right, and see who is running with you. God has a funny way of proving Himself faithful when He is our supreme delight. He will put that special person in your life when the time is right. Trust in His timing; He's always right.

Praying For Your Future Spouse

Josh, a staff member at my youth group, taught me about praying for your future spouse. For one, it demonstrates dependency upon God. And two, it builds your heart full of love and devotion long before the Lord brings the two of you together.

Praying for your future spouse is an excellent method of personal reflection. However, in this dilemma, you are not the only one who benefits. The love of your life will be blessed just as much—arguably, more—than you will!

Now, writing prayers for your future love is a tad different than a straight-up prayer journal. It is an accumulation of messages to your future spouse that you will give to them on your wedding day. Think about them as love letters. Be honest. Be goofy. Be yourself. Your purity is the greatest gift you could give to your spouse, but a close second would be your prayers—preserved by integrity and faith all the way up to that fateful moment.

Here are some starting points:

- Record your prayers for him or her.
- Share the trials you are facing and the lessons God is teaching you.
- Communicate as if you were talking to him or her real time.
- Share funny stories.
- Declare your love for him or her by pledging your integrity.
- Write about the aspirations you hope to have as a couple.

Written text has a compelling way of speaking to the heart. The

time to start loving your spouse is not on your wedding day, but in your everyday conduct. And what better way to do that than by saying, "*I loved and thought about you long before I met you*"? You are going to spend the rest of your life together, so you might as well start working on those communication skills now!

A Letter to My Sisters in Christ

> *Charm is deceitful, and beauty is vain, but a woman who fears the LORD is to be praised.*
> —Proverbs 31:30

Dear Sister in Christ,

Let me first clarify that I am not the perfect guy. As I mentioned, my greatest folly was not being intentional with girls, and it is an area I still struggle in. However, this does not nullify the fact that I deeply care about my sisters in Christ.

The idea of possibly having to raise a daughter in this culture is terrifying; a society where the size of a girl's chest is more important than the size of her heart, where movies tarnish the value of purity, with a music industry that listens to Lil' Wayne on "how to love." Above all, we live in a culture that tells girls they are never good enough.

These are lies fresh out of hell.

As a brother, I beg of you, do not find your identity in the lies of society. Instead, find your identity in Christ. He not only calls you "fearfully and wonderfully made," but He also proved His claim by dying for you. "*Greater love has no one than this, that someone lay down his life for his friends,*" Jesus said (John 15:13).

I have climbed the tallest mountain ranges of the Korean Peninsula. I have witnessed a breath-taking sunrise over Victoria Falls. I have held lion cubs in my arms while exploring South Africa's savannas. However, these natural wonders aren't half as radiant or beautiful as my sisters who fear the Lord.

What makes them so stunning? Modesty sets them apart; a girl who respects her heart and body challenges others to live with integrity.

A heart for others makes them shine; a Proverbs 31 woman unveils a delicate, life-giving spirit that the world desperately needs to see. Above all, a woman whose soul is found in Christ reflects the beautiful, captivating heart of God.

Ladies, men make terrible substitutes for God. If a man has not experienced God's love for himself, he is never going to be able to love you the right way because God himself *is* love! Likewise, you will not be able to experience an intimate relationship with another imperfect human being if you do not know love yourself. If a guy pursues a relationship with you, do not just open the floodgates of your heart. Make him realize what type of man it will take to win you over. He should treat you like the crown of creation the Bible says you are.

If a guy says you must do a certain act for him to love you, he is not a real man. If a guy raises his hand to threaten you, he is not a real man. If a man does not love you for who you are, he is not only a real man, he does not deserve you. What does a real man look like? According to Ephesians 4:13, true manhood is found in the one who loves the Son of God and stands firm in knowledge and obedience to His word. Only through Christ and His word will a man be able to treat you how you deserve.

As a brother, I want to let you know that the way you dress has serious influence on us guys. Men are visually wired. When you wear clothes that reveal, enhance or highlight certain body parts, it becomes difficult for us to keep our eyes on your heart. The fact that we are attracted to the feminine body is not bad in and of itself; however, sin has distorted our desires. Yes, we have a responsibility to conduct ourselves with integrity. However, when you dress modestly, you help us tremendously.

The next time you are getting ready for school, consider the message you are sending with your outfit. Take the analogy of a business. Businesses specifically market their product to their audience. Girls (and us guys!) do the same thing whether they realize it or not. The way you market yourself determines the audience you are going to attract. All girls want to be treated like ladies; however, not all girls dress like ladies. Will your outfit attract the gentleman with the qualities you desire in a future husband? The intimate parts of your body are so precious that only one man should lay his eyes on them, the man who will lay his life down for you under Christ's covenant of marriage. Modesty is not about hiding yourself, but revealing your dignity. It's about asking yourself, "How am I going to use my beauty?"

Again, I'm not saying that I am the model of a Godly man. My desire is to be an encouragement to my sisters amidst a crooked and twisted generation. You are a precious pearl of God's creation, pursued by a loving Savior. I pray that these words inspire you to find a greater sense of identity in the Lord.

Sincerely,
- D. Kim

"A woman's heart should be so hidden in God that a man has to seek Him just to find her."
—Max Lucado

A Letter to My Brothers in Christ

Until we all attain to the unity of the faith and of the knowledge of the Son of God, to mature manhood, to the measure of the stature of the fullness of Christ.
—Ephesians 4:13

Dear Brother in Christ,

Men are in positions of leadership. It does not give us more significance than our counterparts; it is simply how God has designed us to reflect certain aspects of His character.

My message to my brothers is similar to what I told our sisters: we must cease to listen to the damning lies of the world. In our society, we are told to be passive and seek the easy way out. As a result, broken families and divorces are becoming the norm.

Your coach yells it. Russell Peter's comedy made it famous. But what does it really mean to be a man? Read Ephesians 4:13-15. True masculinity is in imitating Christ by remaining firm in His truth—not hooking up with attractive women, smoking cigars, or putting up the heaviest bench press. Phil Johnson says:

> "That's the main mark of true manhood Paul singles out: doctrinal stability—and along with that are some clear implications: you need to be certain of what you believe. You need to understand it. You need to be able to defend it against everything—ranging from the changing winds of whatever happens to be in style at the moment all the way to human trickery and the cunning craftiness of Satan himself. Because the enemy will offer all kinds of counterfeit doctrines that look good and sound OK—false doctrines where the error is so carefully nuanced it's hard to put your finger on what's wrong with it. He will tempt you to set aside what is precise and carefully defined in place of dumbed-down doctrinal formulas that don't necessarily sound dangerous —but are."[xvii]

Integrity must set us apart, in our studies and in what we view on the computer. A gentle confidence needs to seep from our conduct. We will hold the door open for a girl regardless of how attractive we think she is. Honor will permeate our actions. Our pursuit will not be based on the size of a girl's chest, but the purity of her heart.

We have to be intentional with girls. Confession: I was not intentional with girls. Casual pursuits were my greatest folly. I led girls on and broke their hearts. I wish I had known what I am about to tell you now. The fact is, girls perceive things differently than guys. To us, it might not seem like a big deal to go out to coffee every Friday. However, the young lady you casually hang out with might think that you are interested in her. You might not find it significant to call her on the phone every night. But beware, the feminine heart longs to be pursued, and you're pushing all the buttons. Maybe you guys hang out a lot and are "just friends," but when a guy and a girl get close, someone is going to develop feelings for the other; it's inevitable. It is how God designed us.

Purity is an everyday battle, my friends. Promiscuity will bombard us from every angle. Therefore, always have that guard up. Place filters on your computer. Have wisdom in your movie choices. Find accountability partners. When a girl in front of you is wearing yoga pants, look the other direction—the *other* direction! We are visually wired, and that is a beautiful thing in a particular context. However, sin has distorted our desires. For that reason, we must harness the truth of God's word so that we can reflect God's design for infatuation. Not only to honor the Lord through your thoughts, but also to honor your future wife.

Your love for your spouse does not manifest on your wedding day. It is already apparent, in your daily conduct. Would your spouse appreciate the videos you watch on the Internet? How would she feel about the way you treat your friends? According to 1 Peter 3:7, neglecting this truth can result in hindered prayers. God has already decided your bride, and if you have submitted to His Lordship, you are responsible for loving her now and for the rest of your life. Do not worry about finding the right person; *be* the right person.

Brothers, this world desperately needs us to step up. I have failed countless times in this endeavor. However, that does not discourage my heart's desire to see us, men, stand up for truth amidst a crooked and twisted generation. You are the pillar of society, the church, and the family. I pray that these words inspire you to find a greater sense of identity in the Lord.

Sincerely,
- D. Kim

Let's Get This Right

Like many of you right now, I had feelings for girls when I was in high school. Most of my endeavors were unsuccessful; however, looking back, I could have avoided heartbreak and misery if I was more aware of these truths; it comes down to whether we are going to control our feelings or let our feelings control us.

The Word of God reveals that these inclinations are only the tip of the iceberg. They unveil a much greater longing, a yearning that can only be satisfied by the Lover of our souls. Time after time, we seek love in all the wrong places—through another imperfect human being.

So let's get this right.

Let's not fall into another destructive cycle. As C.S Lewis said,

"We are half-hearted creatures, fooling about with drink and sex and ambition when infinite joy is offered us, like an ignorant child who wants to go on making mud pies in a slum because he cannot imagine what is meant by the offer of a holiday at the sea. We are far too easily pleased."

High School is a cornerstone to the rest of your life. The disciplines inherited now will affect your conduct as an adult. Those who are married spend the majority of their lives together; we need to take our relationships seriously.

High school students today have all sorts of reasons for dating.

Because he is hot. Because she is cute. Because he is athletic. Because she is funny. Because of his personality. Because of her accent. Because of how he puts ketchup on his cheeseburger. Because of how she pets your cat. Who knows? I find attractive qualities in several of my friends, as I'm sure you do. But is attraction enough justification for such a significant bond? Attraction is necessary, but it is poor justification for the purpose of dating: to find someone you want to spend the rest of your life with. It is great that she is a good dancer, but does that mean she might be the person you want to spend the rest of your life with? He is not like all the other guys you have met? Awesome. But does that mean he would eventually be a good father to your kids? We must observe the much larger scope. This is the person who will have as much, or more, influence on your life, than your parents. This is the person who will be a parent to your future children. This is the person you will be with unto death. And this is the person you are looking for when you date.

So we're talking about the person you will potentially spend the rest of your life with. I don't know about you, but I don't want to try to figure that out, because I will most likely screw it up. Fortunately, I do not have to figure it out. When talking about someone who will be that significant in my life, I want no one else but the Creator of the cosmos to plan my love story. He is more than qualified for the job.

Dating somebody will never be the answer to all your problems. The most important relationship you could have is a relationship with God. He knows you better than your future husband or wife ever will. You don't have to find your soul mate in high school. There are stories of high school sweethearts, but do not be fooled; these arrangements are not as popular as you would like to think.

Don't let the story of the 40 year-old virgin frighten you and cause you to rashly throw your heart to whoever fancies it. You have much bigger things to focus on, like where your classmates and teammates are going to spend the rest of eternity. As Jesus says, seek first *His* kingdom and *His* righteousness, and all these things will be added to you (Matthew 6:33).

The perfect guy or flawless girl does not exist. For that reason, may we never put expectations on others that we would not put on ourselves. Do not try to find the right person.

Be the right person.

Chapter Ten
One of the Most Powerful Forces in the Universe

Black holes, gamma ray bursts, LeBron James on a fast-break, you know what else is up there? Sex.

Watch the latest movie, tune in to the top ten on iTunes, listen to your friends at the lunch table, and you will hear firsthand how society has tarnished this incredible gift. Sex is treated as nothing more than a fun activity. No one looks forward to the sex talk. But if we are dealing with one of the most powerful forces in the universe, it has to be addressed.

What is the big deal about sex? Its purpose: to unite a man and a woman as one flesh. Think about that for a second: two human souls, each with unique personalities and talents, uniting as one. We are talking about powerful, supernatural stuff. The choices you make about your virginity and sexual purity are some of the most life-impacting decisions you will make.

Too often, churches solely emphasize the repercussions of sex and neglect to communicate its value. When sex is talked about, it's in the context of teenage pregnancies, date rape, or Coach Carr from Mean Girls, "Don't have sex, because you will get pregnant…and die!" While these accounts hold some truth, they only represent half of the story. The deceiver would love for us to think that sex is nothing but a commodity, but he would also love to trap us into thinking that sex is not all that it is cracked up to be. All of this could not be farther from the truth. Sex is awesome. Sex is amazing. And you can quote me on that. Not because it's what I think, but because it's what the Bible says.

The Bible says that sex was created for the exclusive context of marriage. But the temptation is so great, and the more you grow up, the more you are tempted by the world's perversions. I remember the locker room talk and spring break stories. Part of me felt like I was missing out. By the time I was a senior, people were shocked to find out I was a virgin. I thought, "Is waiting really all that it is cracked up to be? Isn't sex something I can at least experiment with?"

> *Flee from sexual immorality. Every other sin a person commits is outside the body, but the sexually immoral person sins against his own body. Or do you not know that your body is a temple of the Holy Spirit within you, whom you have from God? You are not your own, for you were brought with a price. So glorify God in your body.*
> —1 Corinthians 6:18-20

The ramifications of sexual relations come mainly through the unseen world. Sex has two different meanings in and out of marriage. For the husband and wife, sex is the ultimate expression of commitment in body and spirit. For two people hooking up at a party, sex is nothing but physical pleasure, no sacrifice, no lifelong commitment. Sex outside of marriage mutates into a travesty with immense consequences.

So maybe you agree that sex should be reserved for marriage. But you may be wondering about "all the other stuff" leading up to intercourse. *"How far is too far?"* Is oral sex, masturbation, or hanky-panky a sin too? Yes. "All the other stuff" is not acceptable, regardless of whether they seem less severe. There is a reason the Bible is so stern about this particular sin.

We so often get caught up in seeking an obscure line between sin and sanctification that we completely forget about grace. Our attitudes

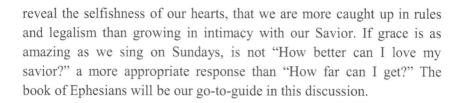

reveal the selfishness of our hearts, that we are more caught up in rules and legalism than growing in intimacy with our Savior. If grace is as amazing as we sing on Sundays, is not "How better can I love my savior?" a more appropriate response than "How far can I get?" The book of Ephesians will be our go-to-guide in this discussion.

> *But sexual immorality and all impurity or covetousness must not even be named among you, as is proper among saints.*
> —Ephesians 5:3

Think of a piece of lint you find when taking clothes out of the dryer. It's a tiny speck of what just occurred the past 30 minutes in that machine. The lint isn't that significant, yet enough of it accumulates to become part of the clothes-drying process. Similarly, not a speck, not a lint, not even the *slightest portion* of sexual sin is appropriate among saints, God's chosen people.

Sulfur and fire are rarely the causes of wildfires. Rather, a wildfire can begin with a half-smoked cigarette or a campfire that is not properly extinguished. A catastrophe can result from a few, seemingly harmless decisions. Ever so more true with sex. One little touch here, or a kiss a little too long, is more than enough to set off the blaze of hormones within your teenage body. Something so tremendous must be reserved for its original intent.

We have already talked about the second part of the verse; it is the message of this book. There is an overwhelming theme throughout Scripture that we are not, in any way, supposed to look like the world. Just as God's chosen people are called to be holy, sex was meant to be holy—set apart for the marriage bed. It is only right that sexual immorality be exclusively treated amongst God's people as if it's as powerful as the Bible claims it to be.

What is so amazing about obedience to God's Word is that we get to partake in its blessings. Following the glory of God is the exaltation of His saints. Many are shocked when they stumble upon the book of Song of Solomon in the Bible. The erotic words of Solomon and his bride reveal that sex is an amazing gift of intimacy that is supposed to be enjoyed between one husband and one wife—*enjoyed!* While complimenting his bride, Solomon is not slow to point out his attraction to her naked body, describing it with phrases such as "two fawns, twins of a gazelle" and a garden which she then invites him to "eat its choicest fruits." Yes, this is in the Bible, and for good reason. Sex is amazing; God describes it in His word with intricate detail. Through this dramatic love song, we observe that God honors pure marital love through an illustration of the spiritual relationship between God and His chosen nation, Israel. The poetry reveals that God is glorified and we are satisfied when His gift is kept sacred. Chastity is a double-win.

God created the penis. God created the vagina. God created sex. He knows what is best. Sex has never been the problem. Sin is always the problem. One-night stands and random hookups are more than a means of self-indulgence, they rip your soul to shreds. Thus, resisting the seduction of the world is a life-giving decision that protects us from the road of regret. Your virginity is a priceless gift to your future spouse. What better way to say "You are the most important person in my life" than by reserving the most intimate parts of your being for the one whom you will spend the rest of your life with.

For those of you who have made a bad decision, be comforted that God is big enough to redeem your spiritual virginity and give you a fresh start. Ask Him for forgiveness. His grace is sufficient for you, and His mercy erases our iniquities as far as the east is from the west (Psalm 103:12).

Purity rings are an excellent, symbolic method of standing firm in the truth. I plan on giving mine to my wife on our wedding day. But I have a proposal for you right here, right now. Below is something I call the pledge. I challenge you as a young man or woman, to take the narrow road in terms of your sexual integrity and signify you are doing so by signing below. This is one of the most important decisions of your life. So, why wait?

I _____ , in accordance to my virginity and purity, pledge to live on the narrow road. Through the power of the Holy Spirit, I will abstain from the temptations of the world that war against my soul.

I acknowledge that sex is God's gift to the married man and woman and will seek to honor that promise through the way I speak, interact, and look at the opposite gender. I understand that loving my future spouse does not start on the altar, but in my daily conduct.

Chapter Eleven
The Narrow Road Through Ministry

And Jesus came and said to them, "All authority in heaven and on earth has been given to me. Go therefore and make disciples of all nations, baptizing them in the name of the Father and of the Son and of the Holy Spirit, teaching them to observe all that I have commanded you. And behold, I am with you always, to the end of the age."
—Matthew 28:18-20

The Mission

I guarantee that none of you will have as haphazard of a college choice as I did.

My final three schools were as follows: Michigan State University, Moody Bible Institute in Chicago, and the University of Pennsylvania. A series of unusual events narrowed my choices down to a school I told myself I would never go to (I was a University of Michigan season ticket holder growing up), one of the top seminaries in the United States, and an Ivy League institution.

I couldn't pass up the opportunity to run track in the Big Ten conference. It was official. Michigan State was where I would spend the next four years. When my friends found out I picked MSU after I had been accepted to Moody, many of them told me something that will always stick with me. "You are being called into ministry." It was amazing that I even got into MBI. Part of my application was lost in the process, and somehow, the admissions office found everything just in time for one last review.

The voices got louder after I declined Bible College to go to MSU.

"You are making a mistake, Derek."

"It is so clear that God has called you into ministry."

What they meant was, "God opened doors for you to attend Moody, so He must be leading you into 'full-time' ministry, as in becoming a pastor or a missionary."

Of course, vocational ministry is a noble task, and God does lead some to serve that way.

But all followers of Christ are "called into ministry."

The mission began the day we dropped our former ways of life and took up our crosses to follow Jesus. As followers of Christ, we are all in the ministry. Just because you are not a pastor does not mean you are not charged to speak truth into people's lives. Just because you are not an overseas missionary does not mean you cannot cross the jungles and swamps of cultural and social norms for the sake of the Gospel. You do not need God to speak through a dream to know you're called into ministry. According to Scripture, every Christian is called into some kind of ministry.

High school is fun, but most importantly, it is a time to get serious about what you believe. It is a time when God can work mightily through you. Friday night-lights, school dances, and quiz bowl provide lifelong memories as well as once-in-a-lifetime opportunities for ministry.

High school is an ideal time and place to do ministry. For seven hours a day, five days a week, you are surrounded by a diverse group of people who are dealing with all sorts of issues. The intricacy makes this period of life unlike any other. It is a breeding ground for future

disciples. My prayer is that you would not see this period as a nuisance but an opportunity for spiritual growth.

Has it ever occurred that it is quite possible that you walk past hundreds of people every day who are hell-bound? I don't want to believe that, but the Bible is clear: the road is narrow, and only a few find it. This predicament calls for action. It demands a mission. What is the mission? What is the objective to accomplish before graduation?

Make disciples and be His witnesses.

The mission is profound, yet original. It's the same as Jesus proclaimed to His followers 2,000 years ago. Just imagine how you would react if someone, whom you saw killed three days ago, rose from the dead and told you to do something. Yet they obeyed, and so must we.

In this chapter, I will offer guidelines to equip you for your specific ministry. We are all called. We are going to talk about disciplines that we must develop in order to be successful at choosing what we want most over what we want now. There are certain truths you must be grounded in before graduation.

The Greatest Story Ever Told

Who? What? When? Where? Why? How? As a journalism major, I have become accustomed to the five W's and H. Before going out on my beat, I review these six points to get a grasp on the nuts and bolts of my story.

The Gospel is the greatest story ever told. Jesus, Son of God, who dwells in unapproachable light, comes down to earth in human flesh to save you and I, filthy, wretched, undeserving sinners, from eternal damnation. He has transformed our lives and given us all a story to share.

Let's look at the five W's of the Great Commission to ensure that we have a grasp on the calling to which we are dedicating our lives.

Who is a Disciple? As a student, you have already experienced, in a sense, what it is like to be a disciple. Disciple simply means student or apprentice, someone who imitates the ways of their "rabbi" or teacher. In Biblical times, disciples lived with their rabbi, learned from him, and imitated his life. For the Christian, the teacher happens to be the Son of the living God. By surrendering our lives and obeying His commandments, we seek to live a life worthy of the calling we have received (Philippians 1:27). Our conduct is an overflow of joy toward the grace we have been shown. We are slaves to Him because we have been bought with a price. Thus, our identity, worth, and security are found in Christ alone. Through faithful obedience, we accompany the Redeemer of mankind to seek and save the lost. Who is a disciple? Anyone who has been born again by the Spirit of God.

What is a Disciple? Think about the twelve disciples.

They were far from perfect. They were ordinary, and in some cases, less than ordinary men. Matthew was a tax collector, and Simon Peter was a fisherman. Not the professionals people tend to look up to. Yet God calls ordinary people to be His disciples—catalysts who change the world for eternity. "Follow me, and I will make you fishers of men." (Matthew 4:19). Disciples do not have to be the smartest, most athletic, best looking, or come from the best family background. They only requirements are availability and uncompromising abandonment.

The bottom line for the Christian is that he or she has been changed. The Christian has been saved from sin and death once and for all and now leads a life of forgiveness and love.

Jesus' Parable of the Unforgiving Servant in Matthew 18:21-35 illustrates how Christians are like the servant who has been forgiven an insurmountable debt. It is comical to believe we could have paid the price for our sins. We are nothing but hopeless wretches in light of God's holiness. Yet, God, out of His grace, still decided to make a way. Oh, what joy should overflow from our lives! We have been given eternal life through a relationship with Jesus. Therefore, may we refuse to follow the latter actions of the servant, who refuses to forgive his fellow servant a fraction of what he has been forgiven.

The disciple, changed by Christ, desires for others to experience the same radical transformation. Love, joy, peace, patience, kindness, goodness, faithfulness, gentleness, and self-control emanate from a desire to see the lost be found in Christ. To keep such a gift to oneself

would be of the worst kind of selfishness. It is only natural to want to multiply.

When Do I Make Disciples? At every opportunity that God gives you.

There is a tragic misconception that disciple-making is reserved for missionaries in developing countries or pastors on Sunday mornings. While vocational ministers adhere to a noble task, the Great Commission pertains to every believer who has counted the cost. It is not an optional consideration.

Some Christians fall into thinking you need to wait until your Bible knowledge is at a certain quota. That's a mistake. God calls all of His followers to make disciples, whether you have known Him for one day or 10 years. Although sufficient knowledge of Scripture is the crux of communicating the good news, discipleship in and of itself is not an acquired skill, but a quest in which you learn as you go.

There will never be a time when you will be perfectly prepared to make disciples.

What matters most is that you are trusting in His Holy Spirit, as you follow His lead.

Discipleship is multi-dimensional; just look at how Jesus modeled it. Sometimes He delivered sermons, but there were also occasions where He ate with and traveled with his disciples. Jesus lived daily life with His disciples by serving them through grace and truth.

Likewise, you can make disciples in everyday life, in the conversations you have after dance recitals or grabbing breakfast with a teammate every Saturday. Maybe it will be through discussions at your lunch table, or giving rides to an underclassman that lives in your neighborhood. Discipleship is sharing the love of Christ through word and deed with the people God has placed in your life.

Where Do I Make Disciples? Your school is your mission field. Where has God specifically placed you within your student population?

Think about your group of friends, team, ensemble, club or workplace. They are in your life for a reason. That reason is for you to tell them about the Gospel. No one has the gateway into his or her life that you have. You have a special purpose in their lives.

God has equipped each of us with gifts and talents to enable us to fulfill the Great Commission. That is why some people are good at 30-foot putts, while others are talented at designing video games. Whatever you are good at, use that platform to be the salt and light of the earth (Matthew 5:13-16). Collaboratively, we can literally change the flavor of the world.

Start where you are planted. I have a passion for the world. I daydream about excursions to the most remote corners of the earth, helping those in need. I get carried away while thinking about my future. However, God commands us to be faithful with little before we are faithful with much (Luke 16:10). Before we take the Gospel to the ends of the earth, we need to start in our "*Jerusalem*" (Acts 1:8). After Jesus' Ascension, the apostles kicked off the mission in their immediate surroundings. Similarly, before we preach the Gospel to the ends of the earth, we need to be faithful where God has us right now.

Why Should I Make Disciples? I'm tempted to reply, "Because Jesus said so." That would be reason enough. But on a more comprehensive level, we should make disciples because it is a natural response.

Imagine you have an incurable disease. You go to every doctor, try every medicine, and it is not enough. Nothing you do of your own effort can shake off this epidemic. But finally, someone introduces you to the cure—at the cost of his life.

This is our story.

Sin is the disease, eternal condemnation is the prognosis, and the blood of Christ is the cure.

If you have been saved from such horridness and have experienced such grace, it only makes sense to want to share that compassion with others.

Paul explains in Galatians 5:1 how Christ sets us free for the sake of freedom. Our freedom from sin is not so that we can bask in all of Heaven's glory for ourselves; we are supposed to bring as many

people as we can with us.

In disciple making, we experience harmony with God unlike ever before because we accompany Him on His mission to seek and save the lost.

How Do I Make Disciples? Making disciples is more than inviting your friends to youth group.

Does that mean you should never invite them to church? Absolutely not. Many have been saved through an invitation to a church service or outreach. But that is not a means to an end. More importantly, that is not a biblical model for discipleship.

Disciple-making involves both the short and long term.

In one sense, it is having the compassion to look someone in the eye and tell him or her about the most important thing in your life. We overcomplicate it sometimes. We get caught up trying to figure out a magic formula for evangelism, when the Holy Spirit provides us with all the boldness we need. The Great Commission starts with opening our mouths. We need to take a break from discussions about upper-body workouts and homecoming dresses, and start telling people about the marvelous gift we have in Jesus.

In another sense, making disciples is building relationships. It is taking the time to build relationships through which the Gospel can be communicated. Words are powerful; however, they are empty if they are not supported by our conduct. Some of these relationships will be with friends you have known since you were in diapers, other relationships began when you just happened to sit next to one other in Spanish class.

The rest of this chapter is dedicated to providing practical pointers on how to carry out the Great Commission in high school. Isn't it awesome that you don't have to wait to be a world changer? For the Christian, every day is a mission trip; every class has an eternal undertaking.

Count the Cost

The road is narrow. Making disciples is no easy task, but it is the supernatural overflow of a redeemed heart. While living for Christ, it is very possible that you might lose some friends. You will definitely be teased; you may be bullied. People will certainly talk behind your back. The Bible says it over and over again. "If they persecuted me, they will also persecute you" (John 15:20). "Indeed, all who desire to live a godly life in Christ Jesus will be persecuted" (2 Timothy 3:12). "Do not be surprised, brothers, that the world hates you" (1 John 3:13).

These warnings of persecution beg the question: is it worth it?

If you have taken economics, you know about opportunity cost. Everything in life has an opportunity cost. And following Jesus is no exception. When you pursue something, there is always an alternative. Is the cost of making disciples worth the investment?

The apostles in Acts 5:17-42 sure thought so. These guys got beaten—physically beaten—because of their faith in Jesus Christ. Not only were they manhandled, but they were also charged by the religious authorities never again to speak in the name of Jesus. Little did the Pharisees know that nothing can restrain Gospel passion. The apostles left the presence of the Sanhedrin Council limping, bruised, probably with some broken bones, yet they rejoiced like the Detroit Lions would if they won the Super Bowl. What could cause such paradoxical joy?

Their reward.

They rejoiced because the joy they had in Christ was worth infinitely more than anything the world could throw at them. *And the same is true for you.* Just think about how awe-inspiring it is that we belong to the King of all Kings, the Lord of all Lords. The sovereign, omniscient, star-making, mountain-moving, sin-bearing, self-sacrificing, I AM WHO I AM calls us His beloved son, daughter, and friend— what?! Yes, rumors about you can be discouraging. It is not easy to have friends, classmates, and teammates taunt the most important thing in our lives. But compared to knowing Jesus, Paul's words in Romans 8:18 speak volumes: "For I consider that the sufferings of this present time are not worth comparing with the glory that is to be revealed to us." And on top of that, as a follower of Christ, you are a part of the Body of Christ— the church—the most unstoppable institution this world has ever seen.

Fellas, when your buddies call you a b**** because you won't pick up the booze, rejoice in the sufficiency of Christ. Sisters, when you

became known as the "prude Christian girl," rest assured in God's blessings of integrity. You can walk into ridicules and sneers with a smile on your face, because you know that the road is narrow, and the eternal reward incomparably outweighs the temporary displeasure.

Unstoppable Movement

When I was young, my family and I attended a Korean church. Korean churches do something that I wish every church did: provide lunch after service. Moms took turns cooking delicious food for the congregation every Sunday. Downstairs in the basement we had a "fellowship hall," where we would eat. The area was also used for youth group, Sunday School, and other gatherings throughout the week. So growing up, this is what I thought fellowship was: getting together, eating, talking, spending time with one another.

Not until I started reading the book of Acts did I realize my conception of fellowship was off—way off.

In a world hostile toward the Gospel, fellowship is your lifeline. It is popular in Christian circles to think fellowship is simply spending time with believers at bonfires or game nights. This is only a glimpse of what God deemed it to be. Fellowship is so much more than Friday and Saturday nights. When you read the book of Acts, you see that fellowship is an unstoppable movement of God.

> *And they devoted themselves to the apostles' teaching and the fellowship, to the breaking of bread and the prayers. And awe came upon every soul, and many wonders and signs were being done through the apostles. And all who believed were together and had all things in common. And they were selling their possessions and belongings and distributing the proceeds to all, as any had need. And day by day, attending the temple together and breaking bread in their homes, they received their food with glad and generous hearts, praising God and having favor with all the people. And the Lord added to their number day by day those who were being saved.*
> —Acts 2:42-47

Now the full number of those who believed were of one heart and soul, and no one said that any of the things that belonged to him was his own, but they had everything in common. And with great power the apostles were giving their testimony to the resurrection of the Lord Jesus, and great grace was upon them all. There was not a needy person among them, for as many as were owners of lands or houses sold them and brought the proceeds of what was sold and laid it at the apostles' feet, and it was distributed to each as any had need. Thus Joseph, who was also called by the apostles Barnabas (which means son of encouragement), a Levite, a native of Cyprus, sold a field that belonged to him and brought the money and laid it at the apostles' feet.
—Acts 4:32-37

"One" and "together" stand out to me as I read these passages. Unity in Christ was what drove the early church to extraordinary accomplishments. Unity shines in the dark world we live in, where most friendships are superficial. To see people from various backgrounds, skin colors, and talents united for one cause is an unusual sight indeed. So deep was the love among the early church that "there was not a needy person among them" (4:34).

Isn't there a part of you that yearns for that kind of community? Friendships are important; there is a time and place to hang out. But living boldly for Christ means being connected to the Body of Christ, people who will celebrate with us in our victories, carry our burdens, and strive alongside us as we press on toward the eternal prize (Philippians 3:12-14).

Finding Fellowship

Dodgeball, throwback David Crowder, and Detroit Tigers sermon analogies. That was the essence of my fellowship in high school. I was blessed to be a part of an amazing youth group called 707. We met on Wednesday nights at 7:07 p.m. for worship, teaching, and small groups. Through Bible studies, mission trips and retreats, I was able to lay a foundation for my faith and meet some of my closest friends. Why is it called 707? No idea. Jack, our youth pastor, didn't even know.

Find a church that has a high school youth ministry. Don't just go to the weekly meetings. Get plugged in. Go on the retreats. Lead prayer groups. Take the initiative. Don't wait for others to take the lead on what God has already called you to do. Your ministry should spur you on to learn more about God's Word while helping you build heart and soul relationships, which is what we are going to talk about next.

Now, I realize not all of you come from a town with three mega churches. My prayer is that whoever you are, wherever you are, you would get plugged into a local body of believers. Your youth group might not be 200 students. It might be 15 or 25 people. That's totally fine. The strength of fellowship is not in the numbers, but in the dedication and zeal of the individuals. Maybe you can't find a youth ministry nearby. If so, why not start something yourself? I was so impressed by a friend who went to a nearby school. Because of the dry spiritual state of her student body, she decided to start a Bible study. She prayed about it, talked to her principal, and it has been going strong ever since. You will be surprised by how consistently God provides other believers to encourage you on the journey when you decide to do big things for Him.

Heart and Soul

Heart and soul brothers and sisters are the essence of Biblical fellowship. They are the people you go to war with. What sets these relationships apart is that Christ is what holds them together. The cornerstone of the relationship is not an after school activity, but the mission that God calls us to. A union so firm that nothing can bring it down. Heart and soul brothers and sisters are duos that change the world for Christ.

Read 1 Samuel 14:1-23.

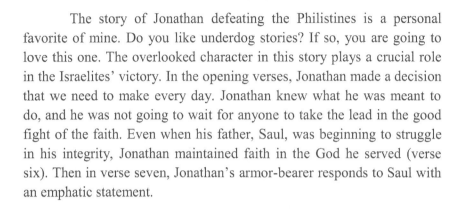
The story of Jonathan defeating the Philistines is a personal favorite of mine. Do you like underdog stories? If so, you are going to love this one. The overlooked character in this story plays a crucial role in the Israelites' victory. In the opening verses, Jonathan made a decision that we need to make every day. Jonathan knew what he was meant to do, and he was not going to wait for anyone to take the lead in the good fight of the faith. Even when his father, Saul, was beginning to struggle in his integrity, Jonathan maintained faith in the God he served (verse six). Then in verse seven, Jonathan's armor-bearer responds to Saul with an emphatic statement.

> *"Do all that is in your heart. Do as you wish. Behold, I am with you heart and soul."*

As we strive to carry out the Great Commission, we need people who are going to run alongside us heart and soul. So ask yourself, do you have heart and soul brothers and sisters in your life? Who are the people you can call at 3 a.m. when your whole world is falling apart? Who is the person who will stand firm with you in your walk with Christ? Who is the friend you can share anything with? We cannot accomplish this mission alone. Heart and soul brothers and sisters will spur us on to much more than we could achieve on our own. That is why it is essential to find a church that has a high school ministry. Because youth groups present an environment where you can begin to develop these kinds of brotherhoods and sisterhoods.

But most importantly, are *you* a heart and soul brother or sister to others? Are you the kind of person someone can call at 3 a.m. when facing a tragedy? Are you someone who encourages others in their relationships with Christ? It's not just about finding the right person, but *being* the right person.

So which group are you going to be a part of?

Are you going to be like Saul, back at the camp, and waiting for someone else to make the first move? Will you follow the Israelites, who hid in the hills, and wait until there's no risk to join the movement of God? Or will you be among the few, heart and soul brothers and sisters,

that strive side-by-side to accomplish what God has called you to do?

What's Your Motive?

As a student, you are encouraged to get involved in all kinds of organizations. Some schools even require a certain amount of volunteer hours to graduate. They look great on a college resume. But what is your real motivation? I'm not bashing volunteering. But don't volunteer for the sake of volunteering. We should always be looking to help others. However, if your motivation is off, your labor is in vain.

Let's make sure that whatever we do, we are truly doing it out of our love for God and for others. We've talked a lot about finding your passion and living it out, finding your sound and playing it loud. The passion God has given you also applies to how you help others. Find your passion, and love others through it. If you love working with animals, work at the humane shelter. If you love kids, help out at a nursery.

Discovering your passions is a big part of high school, and a lot of it happens outside of the classroom. Get experience. Don't just volunteer for the sake of logging hours. Volunteer to love others through your talents. It also doesn't hurt that you will gain experience in the things you are passionate about.

The Most Important Discipline

"What is the most life-changing experience you have ever had?"

This is a common question I get when I play 20 Questions. I had the chance to experience some pretty cool things in high school. Standing before the majesty of Victoria Falls, leading hundreds of my peers in worship, and asking Taylor Swift to prom at her Fearless concert will always be among my most unforgettable memories. However, my answer is simple. My most life-changing experience happens every day, usually in the mornings before school, sometimes in the afternoon, as I spend uninterrupted, alone time with my Savior.

When I decided to follow Christ in seventh grade, Steve, my

youth pastor, sat me down and taught me how to get alone with my Bible. Retreats, lock-ins, and conferences were great, but the most important lesson he stressed was communing with God through the transforming power of His Word. Quiet times have been working miracles in my life ever since. By the time you graduate, and even before then, you need to be able to answer the same question Jesus asked His disciples.

> *Now it happened that as he was praying alone, the disciples were with him. And he asked them, "Who do the crowds say that I am?" And they answered, "John the Baptist. But others say, Elijah, and others, that one of the prophets of old has risen." Then he said to them, "But who do you say that I am?" And Peter answered, "The Christ of God."*
> —Luke 9:18-20

What you just read is life's most imperative question.

Your answer to the latter question of Luke 9:18-20 will determine your eternal destiny. Notice the transition in Jesus' questioning. He was aware of what the crowds thought about Him. But He was more concerned with the genuine response of His disciples. The answer to this question indicates the true condition of one's heart. He does not ask us, "Who do your parents say that I am?" or "Who does your pastor say that I am?" He wants to know who *you* say He is. And we are not going to be able to honestly answer this question unless we are spending uninterrupted, alone time with God in His Word.

Two Jehovah's Witnesses came to my door as I was working on this section. When I saw them through the window, I was tempted to ignore them. But I could not let a witnessing opportunity pass. They were nice people, but my heart broke to see false teaching pervert their perception of Jesus. One thing always stands out when I talk to false teachers: they rely on an outside source to teach what Jesus has already revealed in Scripture. The result is a Gospel twisted by cultic concepts. This elderly couple stood on my front porch and tried to convince me

that Jesus was Michael the Archangel, something that is clearly contradictory to Scripture. I asked them to turn to Hebrews 1, where the author explains how Jesus was greater than the angels. Then I had them read Jude 9, where Jude explains that Michael did not have the authority to rebuke Satan, which Jesus did on numerous occasions. "You only believe those things because someone told it to you," I replied. Just when I was about to talk about the incredibility of the Watchtower, they said they had to carry on with their door-to-door operations, even though my street was already crawling with their counterparts. I presumed I had scared them off.

I am tempted to be proud of what I just did, but my encounter is a reminder of how we must resist the temptation to solely rely on someone to spoon-feed us God's word. As heartbreaking as false teaching is, we can easily fall into the same trap if we are not careful. Ask yourself, are your beliefs really your own? Like a young woman awaiting the response of her fiancé, Jesus wants to know that your love for Him is personal. It would be heartbreaking for Him to hear that your love is merely a reaction of what someone told us to do.

I am not saying we should not listen to our superiors. There is a time and a place to sit down and be taught. But, above all, our response to Jesus' question in Luke 9:18-20 will be rooted in our time alone with Him in His Word. Should you attend retreats? Yes. Should you make it a habit to attend church every week? Absolutely. Gathering and being encouraged by fellow believers are essential to our journey. On a task as daunting as disciple-making, we need to ensure we are intentional about being filled. Develop the habit of weekly church attendance. But, if the pastor's sermons do not result in a personal zeal for the Word of God, then our beliefs never become our own. They are just theories someone told us to believe. And we will never be able to make disciples if we do not have a genuine faith of our own. Jesus wants each and every one of us to respond to His calling. Refuse to just go through the motions. By owning your faith, you decide to do church right. You refuse to just *go* to church, but also *be* the church.

The key is being intentional. When I miss out on my time with God, it is usually because I was not deliberate about it. For example, you know what time you have English class tomorrow. You also know when and where you have to be for tennis practice. Some of you know your schedules weeks or months down the road! Likewise, we need to be all the more intentional with our alone time with our Savior. Set aside a time every day where you will intentionally get alone with your Bible. Stick to the same area so that it becomes routine. Perhaps a cup of tea will help. No big deal if you miss a day. Just start back up tomorrow. Turn your phone off, and realize that you get to commune with the Creator of the aurora borealis and hydrogen peroxide. It will be the best and most valuable 20 to 30 minutes of your day—guaranteed. Do you want to experience the supernatural? Do you have a desire to be changed from the inside out? Then get alone with the Word of God, and read it for yourself. It all starts here.

Don't overcomplicate the Christian life. Read the Word. Study the Word. Memorize the Word. But most importantly, joyfully obey the Word.

One more thought! Prayer journaling is a phenomenal addition to your alone time with God. In fact, I am going to say it is a must.

God is doing significant work in you during this period of life. You might not be able to tell right now, but that is how the Spirit usually works. Silently, desiring childlike faith from His followers. Here's the thing, though. By writing down your prayers, thoughts, concerns, and whatever else is on your mind, you will get a glimpse of what God is doing in the unseen world. You will be able to look back at your journals, many many years down the road, and marvel at God's faithfulness.

As the nation of Israel welcomed Moses' successor, God gave His people a commandment: *remember My faithfulness*. The Israelites were not in the Promised Land yet, and the road ahead of them was long and treacherous (sound familiar?). Things were going to get tough, so God made sure encouragement would remain an utmost priority. Read Joshua 4. Verses 21 to 24 are what I want us to focus on:

> *And he said to the people of Israel, "When your children*
> *ask their fathers in times to come, 'What do these stones*

*mean?' then you shall let your children know, 'Israel
passed over this Jordan on dry ground.' For the LORD
your God dried up the waters of the Jordan for you until
you passed over, as the Lord your God did to the Red
Sea, which he dried up for us until we passed over, so
that all the peoples of the earth may know that the hand
of the LORD is mighty, that you may fear the LORD
your God forever."*
—Joshua 4:21-24

This decree did not cease after the waters of the Jordan returned
to its banks. God demands that we remember His faithfulness today and
every day. Every prayer you write down is much like the memorial
stones the Israelites were commanded to pick up. At first, they may seem
like common objects, but later they become powerful symbols of the God
you serve.

When I think about some of my favorite rocks in my collection, I
cannot help but think about my friend, Allie—one of the first people I
met when I moved to Novi. Allie was smart and captain of the cheer
team, but she also had her fair share of trials. In high school, Allie was a
partier. In her own words, she has done "incredibly stupid things in (her)
life." Time and time again, I tried sharing the Gospel with her, and time
and time again, the response was the same: "I don't want that. I don't
need that." The Holy Spirit put it on my heart to pray for Allie's
salvation. So every time I shared the Gospel with her, I made a note in
my prayer journal. But if I were to be honest, I doubted. "Really, God?
She seems pretty far gone. It would take a miracle for her to come to
Christ."

Yes, it would. And did.

Midway through the spring semester of my sophomore year of
college, Allie gave me a call. The four words I heard still ring in my ear
as a sweet symphony of God's faithfulness.

"I've been born again."

Allie had just gotten back from a retreat that weekend where she
made a decision to follow Jesus Christ. A close friend of ours was going

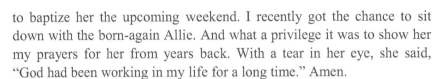

to baptize her the upcoming weekend. I recently got the chance to sit down with the born-again Allie. And what a privilege it was to show her my prayers for her from years back. With a tear in her eye, she said, "God had been working in my life for a long time." Amen.

If you look back in my prayer journal, you will see the answered prayers, but you will also see questions, fears, and doubts. God loves putting us in situations where He gets to display His glory. Contrary to popular belief, He *does* give us more than we can handle, so that He can teach us to trust Him completely.

God does not always answer our prayers as we would like Him to. Many prayers may never receive a clear answer; however, that does not change the fact that God is faithful. He is working every minute detail according to His sovereignty.

Journaling is about being honest. He already knows every thought that goes through your head. Why try to hide anything? We are the only ones who miss out when we decide not to be completely open with God. As dependent human beings, we need to be reminded that nothing in front of us is a match for the power of God behind us. The Israelites had their memorial stones;

what are yours?

- Take a trip to your local bookstore; most have a journal section. Look for a journal that is not too small, not too expensive, and seems convenient to write in.
- Don't forget to write the date in your entries!
- Journal as you spend alone time with God; write down what He is revealing to you through His word.
- Write down your prayers, long and short; think of them like letters to God.
- Follow that Holy Spirit inspiration. If you are dying to write a thought down, do it quickly so you do not forget. Your journal and Bible are your two inseparable companions.
- Some people like to take sermon notes in their journals; others like to keep it solely for personal thoughts. See what you prefer.

- You do not have to journal every day. If you want to, great! You just never want something so intimate and special to become a chore.
- Look back and marvel at the Lord's faithfulness.

Practical Evangelism

Disciple-making requires building relationships, but it also entails sharing your faith in a hostile world. It's scary, I know. To be honest, I would rather not go up to people and talk to them about Jesus. I do not like rejection, and part of me is nervous about how they will respond. But the times I have gone out on a limb and trusted the Holy Spirit are the times I have experienced God in the craziest ways.

I am a big fan of the 10-second rule. No, not the one that has to do with dropping food. Rather, if you ever sense the Holy Spirit is urging you to do something, do it within the next 10 seconds, or you will likely talk yourself out of it. I have learned that you always regret ignoring God's whispers. He never commands us to do something that is not possible without His help. The Spirit of Jesus Christ convicts us of our sin (John 16:8), intercedes in our weaknesses (Romans 8:26), and is our promised helper (John 14:26), but He also strengthens us in sharing our faith.

> *He said to them, "It is not for you to know times or seasons that the Father has fixed by his own authority. But you will receive power when the Holy Spirit has come upon you, and you will be my witnesses in Jerusalem and in all Judea and Samaria, and to the end of the earth."*
> —Acts 1:7-8

I acquired my United States citizenship the summer before my senior year. I did not realize how significant it was at the time. I was just content that I no longer had to deal with immigration services every time I flew internationally. As I sat waiting in the courtroom of the U.S.

Citizenship and Immigration Services in Detroit, I began to feel that Holy Spirit itch. Amidst a smorgasbord of ethnicities, there was only one person I felt I could relate to—and it had nothing to do with his skin color. He happened to be sitting right next to me, the only person in that room who was remotely close to my age. "You should tell him about Jesus," the Holy Spirit whispered.

"What?" I replied. 10, 9 … "At a citizenship office?!" 8, 7 … "He probably doesn't want to be bothered." 6, 5 … "*sigh*" 4, 3 … "Okay, fine." "Hey man, my name is Derek."

"Oh hey, my name is Jesus."

Not sure if there are any responses more appropriate and ironic than that. Jesus (pronounced "Jesús" in the native Spanish) and I struck up a nice conversation. He told me he was Catholic and grew up going to church. I asked if he attended church on the weekends, and he said he went to a church in the town next mine. My new friend Jesús lived 10 minutes away from me, went to my rival school, knew many of the people in my youth group, was the same age as I, and was getting his citizenship moments after I was.

God sure does have a great sense of humor.

That night, we had a big outreach planned at 707. I asked if he wanted to come. It so happened that Jesús had heard about 707 and wanted to come out; all he was waiting for was someone to go with. My new friend ended up coming to church that night to hear the Gospel. We remain friends to this day. He was even in my freshman year writing class at MSU.

I don't know what Jesús got out of that night. But I know God wanted him at 707. The Lord had that encounter planned out long ago. To the Christian, there is no such thing as a coincidence. Every unexpected circumstance is a divine appointment. Jesús and I ended up getting our citizenships the same day not by accident, but as part of God's plan. We wouldn't have connected if I had not surrendered to the Holy Spirit in those 10 seconds sitting in the courtroom. And I'm so glad I did. I am not a fan of clichés, but there is truth in the idea that "life begins at the end of our comfort zone."

Aside from discipling me as a young believer, Pastor Steve also

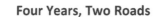

taught me how to play guitar. He was very patient with me, whether I was struggling with insecurity or bar chords. If it was not for his selflessness, I would have never been able to lead my peers in worship my junior and senior years at church. A few hours prior to my last night at 707, the Holy Spirit put it on my heart to thank Pastor Steve. After all, if it wasn't for his work in my life years ago, that evening would have looked a lot different. The thought came at the most random time, as I was checking out at the local bookstore. 10, 9 … I fumbled around in my pocket looking for my coupon. 8, 7 … I remembered I still had to print off my sheet music for the night. 6, 5 … "Crap, I forgot to buy my parents an anniversary card." 4, 3 … I pull out my phone. Another note about the 10-second rule: obey before the craziness of life diverts your attention. I do not remember the entire conversation, but I do recall my last words. "Thank you so much, Steve. The seeds you planted in my life are still bearing fruit today to bless others."

We met about a year and a half later to grab bubble tea. It was the first time I saw Steve since that conversation. "Do you remember that phone call you gave me almost two years ago?" He asked as I took my last sips of my strawberry smoothie. The only thing I could remember about our conversation was that I felt led to encourage him that day.

Bombshell coming up. My phone call that day caught Steve in a fragile period of his life. He held the phone, with me on the other end, in one hand, while his other hand was packing up his office. He was preparing to resign. He was not seeing much fruit in his ministry and thought it was time for something new. Because of the words the Holy Spirit gave me that day, he decided to persevere. I was speechless.

Isn't God's timing the best? You can never underestimate a simple act of obedience. The Holy Spirit goes before us in our efforts. When trusting Him, we can rest assured that no matter how radical or futile an action may seem, He uses our obedience to build His kingdom.

Sharing your faith will not be an option in Heaven. It is a duty strictly reserved for our time on earth. Evangelism does not have to be intimidating; it can be practical with a couple pointers.

First, Start Where You Are Planted. In the Great Commission, Jesus commanded His disciples to get the Gospel to Jerusalem, Judea and

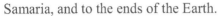
Samaria, and to the ends of the Earth.

Let's break this down. Your Jerusalem is your immediate surroundings: your school, subdivision, or dance studio. Jesus first commands us to spread the good news right where we are. Judea and Samaria were surrounding territories, north and south of Jerusalem. For you, this may be a short-term mission trip to Tennessee, or spending your spring break on the beaches of Panama City, Florida telling people about Jesus.

Finally, we are to get the Gospel to the ends of the earth. It is only because of people who took this last part seriously that you and I are having this conversation, 6,000 miles away from Israel. Whether it is Mozambique, Bolivia, Nepal, or Poland, our God is a global God. We must make it a priority to spread the good news to the vast corners of the earth.

I want to point something out. Jesus gave this commandment in Galilee, where most of His followers were from (Matthew 28:16, 1 Corinthians 15:6). Before we preach the Gospel in Malaysia, we must not forget about our closest friends and family who do not adhere to the truth. A big God means a big mission, and we must be faithful with little before we are given the opportunity to be faithful with much. We do not suppress the former parts of the Great Commission, but we realize we have to start where we are planted.

Who are some of your closest friends who are not Christians? What about your lab partner? Does he or she know about the most important thing in our life? Write down your top 10 closest friends; think about whom would be most open to talking about Jesus, and start going down the list. You don't need to have the entire cafeteria converted by the end of the week, but start with the people at your table. Don't worry about the girl's side of the swimming team if you are unfamiliar with the spiritual state of the guys. God has already given you connections with certain people, and that is where you need to start, the first step in this marvelous mission.

Second, Tattoo the Gospel on Your Heart. You cannot go to war without a purpose. In 1 Peter 3:15, we are told to be prepared "in

season and out of season." In other words, just like my football coach used to say, "there is no offseason" in terms of evangelism. We need to be prepared at a moment's notice to share the Gospel, which means we must be highly attuned with Scripture. If you need a refresher, flip to the Gospel presentation in the latter pages of the book. I highly recommend memorizing the key verses.

Third, Pray Like You Breathe. In 1 Thessalonians 5:17, we are commanded to "pray without ceasing." All the more necessary when we are sharing the good news with somebody. When you enter a room, ask God, "Who is someone I could share the good news with today?"

In every encounter, be attentive to the Spirit's voice. Do you sense an opportunity to direct the conversation to Jesus? If you sense that someone resents the Gospel, then pray that the Holy Spirit would soften his or her heart. If you notice curiosity, pray for a Spirit of conviction. Prayer is the Christian's lifeline. Commune with the Spirit fervently and ask Him to give you the words to say.

Fourth, Time and Place. Ecclesiastes 3:1-15 explains that there is a time and place for everything. This does not nullify the fact that we need to be prepared in season and out of season to share the Gospel. The point is, there are certain situations that are more viable for Gospel presentations than others. Making disciples does not mean we yell Bible verses at people in the hallway, nor does it require us to be any weirder than we already are as Christians. We love people through word and deed first and foremost. On top of that, we listen to the Spirit for opportunities to spread Gospel seeds in our everyday lives. Be wise in your discernment, trust the Holy Spirit who lives in you, and He will open your eyes to divine appointments every day.

Finally, It's All About Jesus. Cliché, I know, but the story of human history is wrapped up in the sentence above. If you don't know how to start the conversation, here is my advice: talk about Jesus. "Hey, man, I know this might be kind of random, but what do you think about Jesus?" That is how I like to get the ball rolling. Ultimately, this is the question everyone will have to answer. As we talked about earlier, your answer to Jesus' question is Luke 9:18-20 determines where you will be forever. Through every gentle word and kind deed, point people to Jesus.

Two Easy Ways to Challenge Your Faith

I had two epiphanies midway through my junior year.

I had just completed the 90-Day Challenge, a Bible study where we read the entire Bible in less than 90 days. I'm not going to lie; it was tough. But the Lord gave me the strength to persevere. During the 90 days, I saturated myself in the Bible. I began to understand the incredible value of God's Word. The Torah comes down to Moses in thunderous fashion on Mt. Sinai, the psalmist in Psalm 119 composes a wonderful 176-verse praise of his love for God's law, and Jesus said in John 14:15 that obeying His commandments is the natural reaction of true faith.

As I read these accounts, I couldn't help but think, "Wow I don't treasure the Word of God *that* much." I kept saying to myself, "If this book is as valuable as Proverbs 16:16 says, better than gold and to be chosen rather than silver, it should never leave my side!" It did not make sense that I carried my phone around with me everywhere, but not my Bible. Something this valuable should not solely be confined to my desk! Keep a Bible in your backpack. Read it on the bus ride home, or while waiting for the bell. I found that just carrying a Bible around led to some awesome conversations. Believe it or not, a lot of people are curious about this book! Instead of letting your Twitter, Instagram, or Facebook app distract you on your phone, let your Bible app 'distract' you! Discipline yourself to open your Bible app more than your email or to memorize a few verses every day. Ask people what they think about the Bible or if they have ever read it. One spark is all it takes to ignite a wildfire, and your Bible may be the start to some life-changing conversations.

Psalm 1 talks about how the righteous person delights and meditates on the law of the Lord "day and night." In other words, always! I pray that through a love for God's Word, you will get to tell others about how He has changed your life.

When I became a Follower of Jesus Christ in 7th grade, one of the first verses I memorized was Romans 1:16, "For I am not ashamed of the gospel, for it is the power of God for salvation to everyone who believes, to the Jew first and also to the Greek." It is disappointing that there have been so many times where I have been ashamed of the Gospel. I can remember countless occasions where I was timid to display my love for Jesus in front of others, particularly through prayer. I would always make it a point to pray before I ate and before I competed, but if I were honest, I would worry about what people thought about me.

"God, thank you for this food (I hope people aren't looking at me) I pray you would bless it to my body (I better hurry up) In Jesus name, amen."

"Father, I thank you for this opportunity to compete today (is the official going to yell at me?) I pray I would glorify you through my performance (did I forget my spikes?) In Jesus name, amen."

Through some major Holy Spirit conviction, I realized that I was more concerned with peoples' thoughts rather than experiencing intimacy with my Star-making Savior. Brother or sister, be bold in your prayer life. 1 Thessalonians 5:17 says our daily lives should be permeated with prayer. Pray before lunch. Pray during practice. Pray as you are walking down the hall. Pray as you poop—seriously! If your friend is upset, ask if you can pray for them on the spot. We do not pray like the Pharisees, who sought the affirmation of men through their religious deeds (Matthew 6:5). Rather, our aim is to be bold, and take advantage of the privilege we have to commune with our Lord. We don't have to go to a priest to have God hear us, or to confess our sins. We can talk to Him whenever we want!

The Savior of mankind calls us friend. We have no reason to be ashamed. He sure was not ashamed of us when He hung on a cross for our sins. Ultimately, we feel embarrassment when we focus on man's thoughts more than God's thoughts. What's the worst they could do to you? Tease you? Abandon you as a friend? Kill you? Awesome. Jesus says your reward is great in Heaven (Matthew 5:11-12). It's a win-win situation for you, my friend.

Not only does God move mountains through the prayers of His

saints, but the watching world may see your faith and become curious. Boldness shines in a world full of superficial ambitions. Be prepared, though: boldness leads to some pretty intense spiritual conversations.

1 Corinthians 13

I had a tough time figuring how I would end this chapter. I mean, how do you top off a discussion about a mission as imperative as the Great Commission? But then I was reminded that our hearts must be in the right place before we embark on this journey.

Why do we take the narrow road? Why do we refuse to follow the lifestyles of the world? Why do we sacrifice time and effort for the sake of making disciples? Love. Jesus. As the Apostle John said at an elderly age, we love because God first loved us (1 John 4:19), and if Jesus is not our true motivation, then making disciples is a waste of time.

> *If I speak in the tongues of men and of angels, but have not love, I am a noisy gong or a clanging cymbal. And if I have prophetic powers, and understand all mysteries and all knowledge, and if I have all faith, so as to remove mountains, but have not love, I am nothing. If I give away all I have, and if I deliver up my body to be burned, but have not love, I gain nothing. Love is patient and kind; love does not envy or boast; it is not arrogant or rude. It does not insist on its own way; it is not irritable or resentful; it does not rejoice at wrongdoing, but rejoices with the truth. Love bears all things, believes all things, hopes all things, endures all things.*
> —1 Corinthians 13:1-7

Without love propelling this endeavor, our actions mean nothing. Amidst all the ups and downs of the narrow road, let us not forget why we do what we do. Here is what I believe to be one of the greatest passages on love in the Bible, articulated by Paul to a struggling church in Corinth.

The Corinthian church was a young church living in a very anti-God culture (sound familiar?). Just to give you an idea, people were sleeping with their moms and tolerating prostitution as part of the worship to their god or goddess (1 Corinthians 5:1-13, 6:12-20). Yes, it was pretty messed up. Paul's first letter to the Corinthians is corrective, providing instruction to a church that is struggling to set itself apart from the world.

In chapter 13, Paul is just getting done talking about spiritual gifts. His point now is that instead of boasting or jealously desiring other gifts, believers should strive to love one another—the greatest gift of all. Some call this the best passage penned by Paul; I would definitely put it up there. Evangelizing, journaling, and carrying your Bible around is great, but before we go out to be the salt and light to our schools, we need to equip ourselves with the attitude necessary for fruitful ministry. As you tell the greatest story ever told through the story of your life, may all you do be done in love.

It sounds so simple, doesn't it? Yet, it is not always that easy. Like we talked about earlier, we need the Spirit of Jesus Christ to guide us into the truth, the truth of Christ-like love. I know I will never be perfect, but I want "love is patient" to eventually be "Derek is patient." Love "does not rejoice at wrongdoing, but rejoices with the truth;" I want the conduct of my life to fit with that verse. In a world that has perverted the meaning of love, people need to see and hear the truth. Love is not soft, harsh, or a happy medium of both. Jesus is love, and love is Jesus (1 John 4:8). He is the reason we do what we do, changed by Christ, we change the world.

Chapter Twelve
Year Four: Senior Year

*But I do not account my life of any value nor as precious
to myself, if only I may finish my course and the ministry
that I received from the Lord Jesus, to testify to the
gospel of the grace of God.*
—Acts 20:24

Senior year! The last year of high school is definitely the best
one yet. The platform you have entering the 12th grade is incredible.
Whether you are the starting quarterback, fifth string point guard; section
leader of the band, fourth chair trombone; president of the chess club, or
first-year member of French club, you have an entire student body
influenced by the way you carry yourself, and you only get this platform
once in your life. My prayer is that you would take seriously the
influence you have on your underclassmen.

Taking the narrow road means living out the opposite of what
the world presents as a typical senior stereotype. Instead of pushing
freshmen into lockers, you should be offering rides to the ones in your
neighborhood. Instead of cutting in the lunch line, you should let others
go in front of you. Remember that Christ—who walked on earth as the

Son of the living God—never chose to exalt himself!

> *In your relationships with one another, have the same mindset as Christ Jesus: Who, being in very nature God, did not consider equality with God something to be used to his own advantage; rather, he made himself nothing by taking the very nature of a servant, being made in human likeness. And being found in appearance as a man, he humbled himself by becoming obedient to death—even death on a cross!*
> —Philippians 2:4-8 (NIV)

Jesus was and always will be the greatest example of humility and grace; those two things go a long way. They are foreign in the world and exactly what your peers need to see. Think about it: you have an entire student body looking up to you. It really is a once in a lifetime opportunity, the opportunity to eternally impact the souls of other human beings, that shouldn't be wasted. Take advantage of every day, every class, every competition, and every moment. What a privilege it is to imitate His humility and grace to students who desperately need Him!

Deciding where to go to college is a big part of senior year. While this topic is dealt with further in the academics chapter, my advice to you is to *"trust in the Lord with all your heart, and ... not to lean on your own understanding. In all your ways acknowledge him, and he will direct your paths"* (Proverbs 3:5-6). Trust in Him one application at a time, one scholarship at a time. He has already gone before you, and His plan is what is best. Don't close any doors He opens, or try to open any doors He closes. Trust me, the Lord might put you in a place where you never thought you would end up! That's how this wolverine became a Spartan!

Realize that going to college really isn't about you at all. It is about God's purpose prevailing in your life. Again, trust Him! He is faithful in each and every circumstance!

Imagine the impact you could have on underclassman through your example. Whether that is helping him with homework or helping her find a classroom, never underestimate the power of a small act of love. Love has an eternal impact when accomplished for the global purpose of Christ. What if your school saw you, a senior, treat others with humility and grace? Humility and grace as a senior? That's uncommon. That's different. That's the narrow road. That's Jesus Christ. Be everyday world changers, starting right where God has placed you. Each day, seize the incredible position of influence you have. You have a once-in-a-lifetime platform to influence your student body for Christ. Now, go finish the mission!

> *I have fought the good fight, I have finished the race, I have kept the faith.*
> —2 Timothy 4:7

May the words of Paul be your own, as you walk down the stage with your diploma nine months from now!

Chapter Thirteen
Good News

This is the most important part of this book.

I would be content if these pages were all you read. Because the Gospel is what the narrow road revolves around.

We've talked about some great stuff in this book. But this last chapter is what the narrow road is all about. The Gospel is the cornerstone of this entire project. The Gospel of Jesus Christ is God's saving declaration to mankind. Don't let the overuse of the word dull its significance. Gospel. We have Gospel music, Gospel choirs, Gospel churches, but what does this six-letter word really mean?

To find out, we need to rewind to the roots. Gospel is the Greek, Septuagint version of the Hebrew word *besorah* that means "good news." Those of you who have responded to the Gospel know why it is so good. At some point in your life, you understood the following: God is holy. In light of His holiness, our sin condemns us to hell. Jesus, out of perfect love, paid the price for our sins. Now, we have a decision to make. Will we remain dead in our trespasses, or respond to God's amazing grace? "Follow me," Jesus says. What is your response?

I don't know why you stumbled across this book, but it is not a coincidence that you did. Could it be that the reason is to hear and respond to the good news? Your response to the Gospel determines your eternal destiny. Some of you, I will know 300 years from now. Others will bear the agony of never-ending condemnation. I pray you would be part of the former. Here is the Gospel: the good news of Jesus Christ. Read it. Memorize it. Take notes. But most importantly, respond to it.

The Gospel Begins With God.

Memorization Verses: Proverbs 1:7 & 9:10

The fear of the LORD is the beginning of knowledge;
fools despise wisdom and instruction.
—Proverbs 1:7

The fear of the LORD is the beginning of wisdom, and
the knowledge of the Holy One is insight.
—Proverbs 9:10

Did you catch that? The fear of the LORD is the *beginning* of knowledge, wisdom, and foundational to understanding the Gospel. Before we talk about the good news, we need to realize Whom we are talking about.

The Bible uses many words to describe God. Love, joy, peace, and light, to name a few. The most important, however, is God's holiness. His holiness is what supernaturally transfigures His other attributes. To say He is holy is to say He is perfectly unique. Completely set apart from anything we have ever seen or comprehended. Right now, in unapproachable light, He dwells in the midst of millions upon millions of angels (1 Timothy 6:16, Revelation 5:11). We would die if we were to see Him in our current state, as he told Moses on Mt. Sinai (Exodus 33:20), because His holiness is too much for our human flesh to withhold.

Let that sink in for a second.

"*I AM WHO I AM,*" the Lord proclaims (Exodus 3:14). He is, He was, and He is to come. God never began to exist and will never cease. He isn't dependent on anything or anyone outside Himself. And even for those who will spend an eternity with Him, one will never completely

160

understand God.

I don't know what I don't know about God. This is a very good thing. Because the Lord is so unfathomable—so beyond us—He deserves our worship. And not only our admiration, but the admiration of every tribe, tongue, people group, and living species on this earth. To understand the weight of the Gospel, you must acknowledge the immeasurable ends of God's holiness.

The Lord created everything—*everything!* Sedimentary rocks, polyester, snorts, Seahorses, the French Alps, electric blue, fast twitch muscle fibers, and us—human beings. He is Creator; we are creatures. He is the potter; we are the pot. We have no right to tell Him what He can or cannot do. When our time on earth is done, and we come into His presence, it's not going to matter what you thought of yourself or if others considered you a good person. Because, among many other things, God is good. And if God is good, then we are not.

Our Sin Condemns us to Hell.
Memorization Verses: Romans 3:23 & 6:23

For all have sinned and fall short of the glory of God.
—Romans 3:23

For the wages of sin is death, but the free gift of God is eternal life in Christ Jesus our Lord.
—Romans 6:23

It's what the Bible says. If you think you deserve the Gospel, then you don't understand the Gospel.

Some of you may think I am mean. That's fine. You are entitled to your opinion. But if my words match up with what Scripture says, your problem isn't between you and me; it's between you and God.

Hell is very real, a place reserved for Satan, his angels, as well as anyone who has sinned against God. It's a place of unimaginable punishment, and our sin has bought us a one-way ticket. Let me make this clear: I don't want you—or anyone else—to go to hell! If it were up

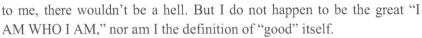
to me, there wouldn't be a hell. But I do not happen to be the great "I AM WHO I AM," nor am I the definition of "good" itself.

Because God is holy and perfect, He must punish sin. If He didn't, He would not be a just God. Imagine if somebody harmed one of your friends or family. Fortunately, he gets caught before he can escape. You go to court, sit through the trial, and at the end, the judge lets the criminal go free. How would you feel? You would be furious. You might even be tempted to take matters into your own hands. Why? Because justice was ignored, and that is wrong. Likewise, at a much grander level, God cannot let someone sin against Him and allow him or her to get away with it.

Many of you will respond by saying you are a "good person," but the Bible says there is no such thing. Sure, you are not a murderer or drug dealer, nor are you anywhere close to the likes of Adolf Hitler, Osama bin Laden, or that stoner in your geometry class. But the humanistic standard is irrelevant in terms of eternity. God's standard is the one true standard. His benchmark is infinitely beyond ours. Of course, you're going to look like a decent person if you're comparing yourself to other depraved human beings. Our standard of good is subjective; God's standard of good is *objective*. He is perfectly good; we are imperfectly not; thus, He sets the rules.

What would happen if you punched your friend in the face? Chances are you two would tussle a bit, but at the end of day, things would end up all right. Maybe. Now let's say you punch the president in the face. What would happen? At the very least, you would get arrested. But it is not too farfetched to presume that a fatal wound could land in your chest from the president's security guards. So what happens when you punch a perfectly holy God in the face? That's the predicament our sin leaves us in. The severity of punishment depends on the one whom is transgressed against.

In light of God's holiness, let's examine ourselves. What if somehow we were able to take every thought that has ever gone through your mind and broadcasted them to your entire school? Every speculation, everything you have looked at on the computer, every word you have said about someone else under your breath.

No one would like you.

Some of you might even get arrested! You don't have to be taught how to sin. It's been that way ever since you were born. No one taught you how to lie, nor did someone have to show you how to disrespect your parents. It was quite the opposite. We had to be taught to tell the truth and how to show respect to others. Human beings are naturally evil. It's unquestionable.

Consequently, we are left in a feeble attempt to fend for our salvation, our ticket to Heaven. But the Bible says our fleshly attempts to be good are repulsive. Isaiah 64:6 compares them to "a polluted garment." Now, that rag isn't referring to a dirty washcloth. Translated from the Hebrew, the "polluted garment" literally means menstrual clothes. So put it like this. Our so-called "good" works are like *used tampons* before God. That says something about His holiness, as well as our sinfulness.

You'll notice that this section is longer than the others; that was intentional. If you're not broken over your sinfulness, you're not going to realize how desperately you need a Savior. His holiness, in contrast with our wretchedness, magnifies the depths of His grace. You see why grace is so amazing when you see how much you don't deserve it. If a mother saw that a semi-truck was about to hit her son who is playing in the street, wouldn't the most loving thing be for her to yell at him to get out of the way? It's not my goal to make you feel bad. I desperately want you to come to a realization of the truth. We are dead in our sins. There's nothing we can do to earn our salvation. If God doesn't intervene, we are in a lot of trouble.

Good thing the Gospel doesn't end here.

Jesus Paid It All.

Memorization Verses: John 3:36, Romans 5:8, 1 John 4:10

Whoever believes in the Son has eternal life; whoever does not obey the Son shall not see life, but the wrath of God remains on him.
—John 3:36

But God shows his love for us in that while we were still
sinners, Christ died for us.
—Romans 5:8

In this is love, not that we have loved God but that he
loved us and sent his son to be the propitiation for our
sins.
—1 John 4:10

While we were drowning in our sin, God looked down and had compassion on us.

He came down to the earth in human flesh through His son Jesus. Prophesized of for approximately 1,000 years, Jesus challenged the false teachings of the day, loved the least of these, and came so that man could have eternal life. Then, in the greatest act of love man has ever known, Jesus hung on a cross—the Roman Empire's instrument of humiliating death—and bore the weight of God's wrath against mankind. Every drop of blood and sweat, every second He endured up on that cross, He endured out of His unconditional love for His children. Thus, the price for sin was paid. Justice was served at the cost of grace. Now, man can find forgiveness and everlasting life by repenting of his sins and placing his faith in Jesus Christ.

I don't know what comes to your mind when you think of the word "grace". It has become a cheap word in our day and age. We say grace before every meal. There's a grace period if we don't turn in our homework on time. But what really is grace? Or better put, *Who* is grace? Jesus. No question about it. Jesus is grace; no further definition needed

Check out Philippians 2:1-11. Do you see the magnitude of Jesus' sacrifice for us? God had absolutely no obligation to die for sinful human beings. The Lord could have chosen not to save anyone, just like He did with the sinful angels (2 Peter 2:4), and it would have been perfectly just of Him. But for a reason we will never fully comprehend, God had mercy on us. In the perfect balance of love and justice, He

poured out His wrath—which was meant for us—on His one and only son.

"Amazing grace, how sweet the sound; that saved a wretch like me." Grace separates Christianity from any religion that has ever existed. A set of rules or a living a "good" life doesn't get you to Heaven. No. Eternal life is only possible through Jesus. Now, through His sacrifice and resurrection, we can have a personal relationship with God.

Can you see what makes grace so amazing?

Follow Me

Memorization Verses: Luke 9:23 & Galatians 2:20

If anyone would come after me, let him deny himself and take up his cross daily and follow me.
—Luke 9:23

I have been crucified with Christ. It is no longer I who live, but Christ who lives in me. And the life I now live in the flesh I live by faith in the Son of God, who loved me and gave himself for me.
—Galatians 2:20

We are saved by grace – period. There is nothing you can do to earn your salvation (Ephesians 2:8-9). Nothing you do will make Jesus love you more, and no mistake can cause Him to love you less. If you are a child of God, Nothing can separate you from the love of Christ (Romans 8:38-39). If you are in Christ, rest assured, brother or sister. You truly have nothing to worry about.

Christians are justified by grace through faith. God no longer looks down on you and sees your sin. Instead, He sees the blood of His son, who ransomed your debt. Now, the Spirit of that God we talked about earlier—holy, omnipotent, omniscient, the great I AM— lives inside of you. In your chest dwells the One who knows the stars by name. As you pursue God through the truth of His word, His Holy Spirit will transform you into His likeness through a process called sanctification. Sin no longer has power over you because you are now supernaturally regenerated "in Christ." These two words have profound implications. You may have grown up without a mom or dad, but "in Christ" you are now a child of God (John 1:12). You might have done some things you're not proud of, but "in Christ" you are now free from condemnation (Romans 8:1). Those closest to you may ditch you because of your new faith, but "in Christ" you are now a part of a global family called the Body of Christ (1 Corinthians 12:27). "In Christ," sin no longer has dominion over you because you are now a new creation (2 Corinthians 5:17). And there's a lot more where that came from.

However, being a Christian does not mean punching a ticket to Heaven and going on to live the same life you did before. Oh, yes, being a Christian does have its privileges (just read all of Romans 8), but there's also a cost to being a disciple. Many yearn for Jesus to be their Savior, but fail to call Him "Lord." But Jesus' gift of grace and our submission to His lordship are inseparable. Following Christ is an all or nothing deal.

Read Luke 9:23-27. Perhaps you have heard a salvation call before. The sinner's prayer, walking an aisle, and raising your hand at the end of a message have become popular ways of inviting people to a relationship with Christ. But Jesus didn't preach or teach any kind of prayer; His salvation call was two simple words: follow me. Jesus commands us to pursue Him, and in the process, deny ourselves. This doesn't mean that it's wrong to have dreams or future goals. What it does mean is that taking up your cross is the acknowledgement that your life is no longer about you. Jesus is your Master, and you are His slave. He can't be our Savior without also being our Lord.

If you claim to know Christ, but don't follow His commandments, I would argue that you are not really a Christian. It's not that works get us to Heaven; it's the simple reality that if you believe something, you're going to act on it. Saving faith isn't through faith *and* works, but works *as a result of faith*. If I showed up to the first day of practice, coming off a summer where I *talked* about how badly I wanted to be a Big Ten champion, but then I ate cheeseburgers every day, partied on the weekends, slacked off in my studies, and took reps off in practice, it would be sound to say that I do not really want to be a Big Ten Champion. Actions speak louder than words, yes? It's not that doing these things boost our chance of getting into Heaven; that's heresy. It's the simple reality that true faith *acts*.

Christianity is about falling in love with Jesus Christ, a relationship not religion. We should be baffled at the fact that this God has pursued us! As a response to the grace we have been shown, we trust and obey His commandments in loving submission.

It doesn't end there.

The believer has hope of future glory in Heaven, where there will be no more death, no more sin, no more cancer, no more broken families; and best of all, we will see Jesus face-to-face. Glorification is the final step of salvation. One day, when Jesus returns to earth, He will *"transform our lowly body to be like His glorious body, by the power that enables Him even to subject all things to Himself"* (Philippians 3:21).

It doesn't end there, either.

The believer will have the privilege of reigning with Christ—*forever* (2 Timothy 2:12). He or she becomes *"heirs of God and fellow heirs with Christ"* (Romans 8:17). It's pretty awesome to be a Christian.

So there you have it: the Gospel.

There will be some bumps in the road. Taking up your cross is no easy task (just look at the latter part of Romans 8:17). We're not going to turn into perfect people overnight. But what matters is that you and I take seriously Jesus' call to follow Him. It is not enough just to intellectually acknowledge these truths. One must make a decision to deny himself and follow Christ.

It's not easy. Never has been. The Bible says the road that leads to life is narrow and difficult. You see, the wide road—the path that most take—is easy. And there's a reason for that. Of course, it would be easier to go along with the crowd and do whatever "feels" good. But, ultimately, what "feels" good does not satisfy. Although following Jesus might be an unpopular route, it's the only way that leads to true significance. He is infinitely worthy of our admiration. And falling in love with Him only leads to good.

I pray that these words give you a more accurate view of the Gospel of Jesus Christ. The road is narrow and unpopular.

But Jesus is worth it—so, so worth it (Philippians 3:7-8).

Chapter Fourteen
The Real King

There is something special about the fall. The changing leaves, cider mills, Friday night-lights, and amidst the excitement is the best event of the school year—Homecoming. I love the way the student body and community come together. Spirit days, parades, the big dance; it is an exciting time, indeed!

At the climax of it all is the coronation of the Homecoming King and Queen. The couple is often portrayed as the pinnacle of high school glory; two individuals selected to represent their student body to an entire community. Occasionally, it is the class crush, other times, the captain of the football team. But my senior year, the story of the Homecoming King became a testament of God's faithfulness. My senior Homecoming will not be remembered because of a game-winning touchdown or a cute date. Instead, October 1, 2010 will forever be a manifestation of how a holy, majestic God uses imperfect, ordinary people in His grand scheme of redemption.

Perhaps my most undeserved merits were the two years I was chosen to be on Homecoming court. I was privileged to be a part of an outstanding group of people my sophomore and senior years, individuals that, quite frankly, deserved the accolade more than I did. Maybe the Homecoming King and Queen are not a big deal at your school. Maybe you think all the hoopla is overrated. But, more often than not, the position holds powerful influence over the community you live in. Because the Homecoming King and Queen is such an esteemed distinction, the Lord put it as a burden on my heart once October approached. I prayed that the Lord would move mountains on my senior year Homecoming court. I asked that regardless of the result, my senior Homecoming would be a time where the name of Jesus would be lifted high.

Being selected myself was a foreign thought. I had the privilege of serving on the court my sophomore year and thought someone else was likely to get a shot when I was an upperclassman. However, God's plans tend to be different than ours. As I walked to Practical Public Speaking following the preliminary round of voting, I was surprised by the remarks I received in the hallway.

"I voted for you, Derek!"

"I told my whole class to vote for D. Kim!"

Over the PA system, Mrs. Lemieux announced the results of the senior homecoming court nominees prior to the 1:55 bell: *"Kaley Bowles, Savannah Green, Alyssa Miller, Marissa Nussio, Joey Ferriss, Derek Kim, Aaron Martinez, and Travis Vincent."* A school-wide vote next week would determine the king and queen. Every night following my nomination, I prayed the same simple prayer before going to bed. *"Lord, glorify your name. I ask you would do something amazing on October 1."*

The big day was a week away, and it was time to get ready. To this day, I still have trouble tying a tie, so you can only imagine the help I needed to look somewhat presentable in the parade. There was one more thing to take care of: telling my coach I would have to miss pregame walkthrough. At this point, my senior football season was not going well. We were sitting at a mediocre record, and the last thing I wanted was my coach to think I was putting my social status above the team. To my surprise, he congratulated me and said it would not affect my position on the depth chart. Things were lining up for God to do something extraordinary.

The parade was grand. Savannah and I had a blast taking pictures

and throwing candy to our family and friends as we were escorted to Wildcat Stadium in a blue corvette. Part of me was sad because it was my last Homecoming, but speculation took precedence over the emotion. *"I wonder what God is going to do tonight. Is He going to answer my prayer?"* By the time we arrived at school, I scurried to the locker room to get my shoulder pads on. The excitement built with every piece of equipment I threw on. The stands were already packed, and I was ready to put on a show for my school and college scouts. *"Better get your popcorn ready,"* my arrogance whispered.

I ran onto the field, joined the closest agility drill, and was immediately scolded by my coach. It was not the usual *"Kim what are you doing?!"* but *"Kim, get your a** off the field!"* That was unexpected. Did I still have my sash on? Were my high-knees really that horrendous? Confused, I ran off the field and into the locker room to seek an explanation before kickoff.

As coach wrapped up his pregame speech, I grabbed my quarterback to see if he had an explanation for the altercation. Hearing his response was like swallowing a rock.

I was benched.

Why? Because coach thought I had elevated my social status above the team. To say I was pissed is an understatement. I was furious that I was benched for what I had clarified with coach a week ago. Was this a cruel joke? Does he just not like me as a person? It did not fully hit me that I was not going to play a down in my senior homecoming game, a highly anticipated matchup that drew the attention of college coaches. Before running through the tunnel, I grabbed my position coach to beg him for possible solutions. His response was dismal. *"I'll do what I can, Kim, but don't get your hopes up."* As my dreams of playing college football became a faint reality, I hunched my head and slowly jogged onto the field one last time.

I was disappointed, but more than anything, I was angry. I felt betrayed. *"Coach told me I would play! I don't deserve this. I have worked harder than anyone on the field,"* my pride told me. Unfortunately, my ego spilt into my conduct on the sideline. While I was usually the one running up and down cheering on my teammates, I decided to be the living, breathing 40-yard line marker for the night. I was not going to budge, not for a teammate, coach, or even an official. To be honest, I was being a complete brat. I wouldn't even give my teammates high-fives as they ran off the field. *"They can get their own water,"* I thought. Disappointed and crushed, I felt animosity begin to build up inside me. It was at this point that I realized I had a choice to make: was I going to feel sorry for myself, or try to find good in my situation? Little did I know that God's hand was at work amidst my pity party.

I closed my eyes and began to pray. What other option did I have at this point? *"Father, why are you doing this? Are you trying to teach me something?"* Suddenly, the crowd erupted. We had scored on an option pitch to take the lead. The score was now Novi 14, South Lyon 11. I looked closer at the scoreboard. 14 to 11. I couldn't get the score out of my mind. *"Those numbers look really familiar."* They were the numbers that appeared in the chapter I read last night.

> *For everyone who exalts himself will be humbled, and he*
> *who humbles himself will be exalted.*
> —Luke 14:11

The book of Hebrews describes Scripture as living and active. Ephesians compares it to a sword, because of its tendency to pierce to the innermost parts of our being. Sharper than a double-edged sword, Scripture slashed truth into my situation that night. While I thought I was the victim of arrogance, I had become the very thing I resented. The Lord opened my eyes to my selfishness. Yes, maybe I had been wronged, but I am not entitled to anything. Who was I to think I deserved playing time? Philippians 2:1-11 was another gash through my ego, as I was reminded of how Jesus, even though He was God, did not count His position something to be grasped, but instead emptied Himself to the point of being beaten to a bloody pulp. Christ deserved everything. We deserve nothing. Yet, He offers us grace. I have nothing to brag about. I was challenged by the Spirit to hand over my situation. There were still five minutes left in the quarter. It wasn't too late to humble myself. For the

remainder of the half, I went from whiner to water boy—and I embraced it. If there was something that needed to be done, I did it, everything from writing statistics to filling Gatorade bottles.

As I sought to serve my team and coaches, I was reminded of another passage of Scripture,

> *"The greatest among you shall be your servant."*
> —Matthew 23:11

Jesus is the supreme, magnificent, omnipotent Redeemer of mankind. Yet, how did He lead? He served. What a paradox! Whether it was in the Garden of Gethsemane before His death, or in Galilee feeding the multitude, Jesus embraced the role of servanthood. I did everything I could to pour myself out to my teammates. Meanwhile, the ball came back into our possession. Our quarterback took a knee to run out the clock, and boom. It was halftime.

At this point, it was hard for me to reign in my emotions. As the team ran into the locker room, I took a knee on the sideline and prayed before the court members would be introduced. *"Lord, forgive me for my arrogance. In a few minutes someone is going to win this thing. One last time, I pray the same prayer that You put on my heart weeks ago: that you would glorify Your name this year on our Homecoming court. In Jesus' name, Amen."*

Even though the Lord was teaching me through the situation, it did not nullify the fact that I was disappointed. By the time I met up with my parents on the 50-yard line, tears were rolling down my face. My mom asked me why I was upset. *"This is one of the last times I will play in front of the home crowd, and the only memory I will have from this night is sitting on the sideline."*

Gently, she told me in Korean, *"You have far more things to be thankful for than things to hang your head about."* Her words were comforting, but I was still hanging on to my discouragement.

As my family and I were introduced to the Novi community, an epiphany erupted in my mind. I was reminded of God's past faithfulness with every step I took toward the bleachers. Me, a first generation Asian

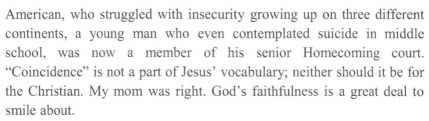
American, who struggled with insecurity growing up on three different continents, a young man who even contemplated suicide in middle school, was now a member of his senior Homecoming court. "Coincidence" is not a part of Jesus' vocabulary; neither should it be for the Christian. My mom was right. God's faithfulness is a great deal to smile about.

After the underclassmen court members were introduced, the friendly voice of Gerry Litman, a former football coach, filled the atmosphere, *"And your 2010 Homecoming King and Queen are...."*

Everything was a blur from that point on.

Evan, last year's king, was the first to congratulate me as he placed his crown on my head. Alyssa and I embraced as the rest of the court came and congratulated us. Then, we took pictures—lots of them; I thought we were going to go blind. *"So this is why people don't like the paparazzi."* The next ten minutes was a joyful period of hugs and high-fives. I remember the cheerleaders, many of whom I had known since middle school, coming up to me and greeting me with a warm embrace. I remember my teammates from the track squad scurrying down from the bleachers to crush me with a team bear hug. I remember greeting parents, and my friends' siblings asking me to take pictures with them. By the time I made it back to the locker room, it felt like every tribe and tongue in Novi had approached me!

I eventually made it to the locker room with just enough time to put my crown away. Tying my shoes, I finally had a second to pause and evaluate the last 20 minutes. *"So, if I won this thing and had prayed this entire month that God would glorify His name on this night, did He answer my prayer?"* I considered several possibilities for a moment, but then realized I had to hurry to prepare for the second half. I ran into the bathroom and quickly splashed water on my hands and feet. As I dried off, a black residue smeared my hands—my prayer was answered.

As I looked in the mirror, I saw smudged symbols of my Savior on my face. Why was I benched the first half? Because God's name had to be glorified. You see, because it was my senior Homecoming game, I wanted to do something special. That week I decided to draw crosses on my face with eye-black. However, as I went through practices that week,

I noticed that the eye-black quickly smeared once I began to sweat, which concerned my plans for that Friday night. However, I had not broken a single drop of sweat in the past few hours. No question, if I had played, the crosses would be smudged and erased by halftime. But that night, the mark of my Savior was clear as could be. All the different groups of people I interacted with, the cheerleaders, parents, siblings, the newspaper, the Facebook pictures, tweets, Instagram pictures, the images in the yearbook, would all see one thing on the face of their Homecoming king: the real King.

I don't think anyone celebrated in an empty locker room as vehemently as I did at that moment. I couldn't believe it! Despite my hard heart, the Lord was gracious enough to display His faithfulness. I cried twice that night: once, because I doubted God's faithfulness, and the second time because He had proven me wrong.

As I strapped on my helmet and ran onto the field to warm-up for the second half, I was taken aback by the star-filled sky of that autumn night. The prophet Isaiah's words flooded my mind as I gazed at God's magnificent handiwork.

> *To whom then will you compare me, that I should be like him? Says the Holy One. Lift up your eyes on high and see: who created these? He who brings out their host by number, calling them all by name, by the greatness of his might, and because he is strong in power not one in missing.*
> —Isaiah 40:25-26

> *For my thoughts are not your thoughts, neither are your ways my ways, declares the LORD. For as the heavens*

*are higher than the earth, so are my ways higher than
your ways and my thoughts than your thoughts.*
—Isaiah 55:8-9

As my high school experience approached its conclusion, I was reminded of the sovereignty of the God I serve, and that despite His splendor, He still uses ordinary, undeserving people like me to further His kingdom. Perhaps the greatest comfort of the narrow road is the knowledge that God goes before us in the endeavor. High school is not easy, but that is okay. Because when we—a generation who seeks the exaltation of Jesus—venture on this road less traveled, we do not journey alone. The King of all Kings accompanies us.

Why take the narrow road? Because God loves to reward those who follow Him. Not necessarily in A+'s or Division One scholarships, but through the surpassing, infinite worth of knowing His Son Christ Jesus. You have the opportunity to play a role in His all-encompassing plan of redemption. As you venture into the future, I pray the narrow road would ultimately draw you into closer intimacy with Christ. The journey is difficult, but the joy you find on the road is never-ending, like the stars in the sky and the One who calls them by name—the King Jesus Christ.

He is worth it!

*You are the light of the world. A city set on a hill cannot
be hidden. Nor do people light a lamp and put it under
a basket, but on a stand, and it gives light to all in the
house. In the same way, let your light shine before
others, so that they may see your good works and give
glory to your Father who is in Heaven.*
—Matthew 5:14-16

[i] David, Kinnamon. *You Lost Me. Why Young Christian Are Leaving Church...And Rethinking Faith*. Baker Books,

[ii] Piper, John. *Don't Waste Your Life*. Wheaton, Illinois: Crossway Books, 2003. 44-45. Print.

[iii] "How Much Money Do Parents Spend on Their Kids?."*Mom.me*. N.p.. Web. 29 Dec 2013. <http://mom.me/mind-body/5089-how-much-money-do-parents-spend-their-kids/>.

[iv] 2003 Environmental Scan, a report to the OCLC membership, "Worldwide Education and Library Spending," Online Computer Library, http://www.oclc.org/reports/escan/economic/educationlibraryspending.htm (accessed March 18 2012).

[v] United Nations Development Program, *Human Development Report 2003* (New Work: oxford University Press, 2003) 92

[vi] "Slavery by the Numbers ." *End It Movement*. N.p., 1 Jan. 2013. Web. 29 Dec 2013. <http://enditmovement.com/learn>.

[vii] MyHealthNewsDaily, . "5 health problems linked to energy drinks." *Mother Nature Network*, Nov. 16, 2012. http://www.mnn.com/food/beverages/stories/5-health-problems-linked-to-energy-drinks (accessed March 23, 2013).

[viii] "Dentists warn of high acidity in some energy drinks. *"Channel 3000*, Feb. 27, 2013. http://www.channel3000.com/news/Dentists-warn-of-high-acidity-in-some-energy-drinks/-/1648/19116630/-/okhqmz/-/index.html (accessed March 23, 2013).

[ix] Keller, Timothy. *The Reason for God: Belief in an Age of Skepticism*. New York: Riverhead Books, 2008. 139. Print.

[x] Psalm 23, Matthew 9:36, Mark 6:34, Isaiah 53:6-7, Romans 8:36-37, John 10:12; 28, 1 Peter 2:25, James 5:19-20

[xi] "Unto you who believe, He is precious." *Gracestoration.* N.p.. Web. 31 Dec 2013. <http://gracestoration.org/>.

[xii] *Alcohol Advertising and Youth, 1997-2007,* www.camy.org/factsheets/sheets/Alcohol_Advertising_and_Youth.html (April 2007)

[xiii] Martin G. Collins, *The Miracles of Jesus Christ: Water Into Wine (Part One), 2006,* http://www.bibletools.org/index.cfm/fuseaction/Library.sr/CT/BS/k/1187/Miracles-Jesus-Christ-Water-Into-Wine-Part-One.htm (November 2006)

[xiv] Hampton Keathley IV, *Turning the Water into Wine, (date),* http://bible.org/seriespage/turning-water-wine, (month, year); Amos 9:12-15, Jeremiah 40:12

[xv] Lifehouse. "Everything." *No Name Face.* SKG Music, 2000. L.L.C.

[xvi] Swift, Taylor and Boys Like Girls. "Two is Better Than One." Pusher Media, 2009.

[xvii] Johnson, Phil. "Growing Up: Becoming a Real Man."*Grace To You.* N.p., 8 Aug. 2011. Web. 31 Dec 2013. <http://www.gty.org/blog/B110808>.

Made in the USA
Charleston, SC
18 February 2014